Diseases and Disorders

Sexually Transmitted Diseases

Titles in the Diseases and Disorders series include:

Alzheimer's Disease
Anorexia and Bulimia
Arthritis
Asthma
Attention Deficit Disorder
Autism
Breast Cancer
Cerebral Palsy
Chronic Fatigue Syndrome
Cystic Fibrosis
Diabetes
Down Syndrome
Epilepsy
Hemophilia
Hepatitis
Learning Disabilities
Leukemia
Lyme Disease
Multiple Sclerosis
Phobias
Schizophrenia
Sexually Transmitted Diseases
Sleep Disorders
Smallpox
West Nile Virus

Diseases and Disorders

Sexually Transmitted Diseases

Tassia Kolesnikow

LUCENT
BOOKS®

THOMSON

™

GALE

San Diego • Detroit • New York • San Francisco • Cleveland
New Haven, Conn. • Waterville, Maine • London • Munich

THOMSON
★ ™
GALE

To Rick, Karu, and Xanda, for an ever-changing and refreshing perspective.

© 2004 by Lucent Books. Lucent Books is an imprint of The Gale Group, Inc.,
a division of Thomson Learning, Inc.

Lucent Books® and Thomson Learning™ are trademarks used herein under license.

For more information, contact
Lucent Books
27500 Drake Rd.
Farmington Hills, MI 48331-3535
Or you can visit our Internet site at http://www.gale.com

LIBRARY OF CONGRESS CATALOGING-IN-PUBLICATION DATA

Kolesnikow, Tassia.
  Sexually transmitted diseases / by Tassia Kolesnikow.
    p. cm. — (Diseases and disorders) (Great medical discoveries)
Summary: Examines the history, diagnosis, symptoms, treatment options, and
prevention of sexually transmitted diseases, as well as ongoing research for a cure.
Includes bibliographical references and index.
  ISBN 1-56006-910-4 (hardback : alk. paper)
  1. Sexually transmitted diseases—Juvenile literature. [1. Sexually transmitted
diseases. 2. Diseases.] I. Title. II. Series. III. Diseases and disorders series.
  RC200.25 .K65 2004
  616.95'1—dc21
                                                            2003002300

Printed in the United States of America

3/05

Table of Contents

"The Most Difficult Puzzles Ever Devised"

C HARLES BEST, ONE of the pioneers in the search for a cure for diabetes, once explained what it is about medical research that intrigued him so. "It's not just the gratification of knowing one is helping people," he confided, "although that probably is a more heroic and selfless motivation. Those feelings may enter in, but truly, what I find best is the feeling of going toe to toe with nature, of trying to solve the most difficult puzzles ever devised. The answers are there somewhere, those keys that will solve the puzzle and make the patient well. But how will those keys be found?"

Since the dawn of civilization, nothing has so puzzled people—and often frightened them, as well—as the onset of illness in a body or mind that had seemed healthy before. A seizure, the inability of a heart to pump, the sudden deterioration of muscle tone in a small child—being unable to reverse such conditions or even to understand why they occur was unspeakably frustrating to healers. Even before there were names for such conditions, even before they were understood at all, each was a reminder of how complex the human body was, and how vulnerable.

While our grappling with understanding diseases has been frustrating at times, it has also provided some of humankind's most heroic accomplishments. Alexander Fleming's accidental discovery in 1928 of a mold that could be turned into penicillin has resulted in the saving of untold millions of lives. The isolation of the enzyme insulin has reversed what was once a death sentence for anyone with diabetes. There have been great strides in combating conditions for which there is not yet a cure, too. Medicines can help AIDS patients live longer, diagnostic tools such as mammography and ultrasounds can help doctors find tumors while they are treatable, and laser surgery techniques have made the most intricate, minute operations routine.

This "toe-to-toe" competition with diseases and disorders is even more remarkable when seen in a historical continuum. An astonishing amount of progress has been made in a very short time. Just two hundred years ago, the existence of germs as a cause of some diseases was unknown. In fact, it was less than 150 years ago that a British surgeon named Joseph Lister had difficulty persuading his fellow doctors that washing their hands before delivering a baby might increase the chances of a healthy delivery (especially if they had just attended to a diseased patient)!

Each book in Lucent's *Diseases and Disorders* series explores a disease or disorder and the knowledge that has been accumulated (or discarded) by doctors through the years. Each book also examines the tools used for pinpointing a diagnosis, as well as the various means that are used to treat or cure a disease. Finally, new ideas are presented—techniques or medicines that may be on the horizon.

Frustration and disappointment are still part of medicine, for not every disease or condition can be cured or prevented. But the limitations of knowledge are being pushed outward constantly; the "most difficult puzzles ever devised" are finding challengers every day.

STDs: A Worldwide Epidemic

S EXUALLY TRANSMITTED DISEASES (STDs), also called venereal diseases, are a varied group of more than twenty illnesses that are classified together because they are passed from person to person primarily by sexual contact. Some, such as syphilis and gonorrhea, are ancient afflictions. Some, notably HIV/AIDS, have been identified only in recent decades. Some cause mild, acute symptoms and some are life-threatening. They are caused by many different infectious organisms and treated in different ways. Together, however, they are among the most common diseases in the United States. Since 1995, five of the top ten most commonly reported diseases have been STDs, representing up to 87 percent of the total reported cases of all ten diseases. STDs are also the cause of growing alarm among the medical and public health community, not only because of their serious effects and complications but because they are spreading at exponential rates worldwide, creating a global epidemic that is presently out of control.

The global STD epidemic is a relatively new phenomenon, but the existence of STDs is not. References to diseases now recognized as syphilis and gonorrhea, the only major STDs prior to 1960, appear in records dating back five thousand years. Both were resistant to countless attempts at cures until the discovery of penicillin in 1928 ushered in the age of antibiotics, the "miracle drugs" that dramatically reduced the danger of syphilis and gonorrhea and by the 1950s led many people to believe the problem of STDs had been solved.

STDs Are a Fast-Growing Epidemic

Beginning in the 1960s, however, reported cases of sexually transmitted diseases were on the upswing. By 1980 eight new STD pathogens had been identified in the United States. Most prevalent were chlamydia, which has since become the most common bacterial infection in the United States, infecting roughly 3 million

A poster from the 1930s touts the curative power of penicillin against gonorrhea, a common sexually transmitted disease.

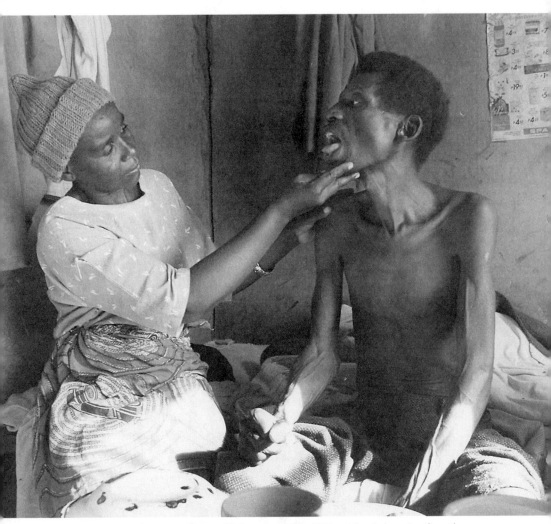

A nurse in Zambia cares for an AIDS patient. The AIDS epidemic has significantly reduced life expectancy in many African countries.

people each year; and genital herpes, an incurable viral STD that epidemiologists now estimate will infect one in four Americans during their lifetime. Researchers also began to identify STDs such as human papillomavirus (HPV) that showed no immediate symptoms and therefore could go undetected for many years while remaining infectious. By 2003 more than 15 million Americans, including 3 million teenagers, were infected with an STD each year.

With limited treatment options available, public health agencies increased STD information and prevention programs, but most people continued to worry more about clearing up the immediate symptoms of an STD infection than about avoiding infection in the first place. Increasingly, however, researchers sounded the alarm that the long-term consequences of STDs were much more dangerous than acute symptoms. HPV, for example, increase the incidence of cervical cancer in women, chlamydia is linked to infertility, and hepatitis C can lead to liver cancer.

In 1981 the scope of STD transmission took on new significance when scientists identified HIV, a previously unknown virus, as the infectious agent in the AIDS epidemic. AIDS was both incurable and deadly, forcing people to consider the risks of unprotected sexual activity as never before, especially after studies indicated that contracting almost any STD increases the risk of subsequently acquiring or transmitting HIV.

As of February 2003, science writer Michael Specter reports, 65 million people have been infected with HIV worldwide, most of them in Africa, and 25 million have died. The AIDS epidemic has undermined the political stability and economies of sub-Saharan Africa and single-handedly reduced life expectancy in Kenya from sixty-six to forty-eight years within the past decade. UN secretary general Kofi Annan has publicly estimated the necessary financial cost of fighting AIDS worldwide at $7 to $10 billion per year.

STDs Can Be Prevented

The scope and severity of the epidemic has also made one message more important than ever: STDs can be prevented. However, prevention depends on knowledge, education, and voluntary changes in human behavior. Limiting sexual activity and sexual partners, using condoms correctly and consistently, and undergoing regular medical screening to diagnose infection are all low-cost, highly effective prevention strategies. Key to the success of these strategies is frank communication about STDs, however, which means overcoming the strong social stigmatization that has traditionally surrounded STDs.

Because openly addressing sexual health and sexual practices is traditionally discouraged in most cultures, the STD epidemic has been referred to as a "silent" or "hidden" epidemic; but the devastating effects of STDs in recent decades have made STDs impossible to ignore. Ignorance, however, is still widespread; as recently as January 2003, a brief issued by the Association of American Colleges and Universities reports that 50 percent of fifteen- to twenty-four-year-olds in key developing countries of the Caribbean, Central Asia, Eastern Europe, and East Asia, where AIDS is fast spreading, have never heard of HIV. Controlling the STD epidemic means educating people, particularly young people, about sexually transmitted diseases and encouraging them to take responsibility for their own health and well-being.

Chapter 1

STDs: A Common Cause for Concern

S EXUALLY TRANSMITTED DISEASES (STDs) are a group of infectious diseases that are passed from person to person primarily by sexual contact. More than twenty diseases are classified as STDs. Their symptoms vary, their severity and effects vary, and they are caused by varied kinds of organisms, so no one description fits all STDs.

It is important to understand that though most STDs involve the genitals, the symptoms and effects of STDs can occur anywhere in the body. Similarly, the appearance of symptoms in the genital area does not automatically indicate infection by an STD. There are many other diseases that affect the genitals, from bacterial infections to cancer, that are not classified as STDs because they are not transmitted through sexual contact.

Besides their common method of transmission, STDs have another important feature in common: They are occurring at epidemic levels in human populations around the world, and the rate of infection is rising sharply, especially among young people. This is particularly bad news because STDs are not merely nuisance diseases. They cause serious and lasting health problems and have huge medical and economic costs.

How STDs Are Spread

The infectious organisms that cause STDs survive and thrive in specific areas on or within the body. A type of tissue known as the mucous membrane is the preferred habitat for most of the microscopic germs that cause STDs. This soft, warm, moist tissue is found within the penis, vagina, anus, mouth, and eyes. Therefore, STDs are usually spread by direct physical contact between an infected person and the genitals, mouth, or anus of another person. Vaginal, anal, and oral sexual activity provides opportunities for the spread of these germs from one person to another. Less direct forms of sexual activity, such as kissing or close body contact, can also transmit STDs through the exchange of saliva or other body fluids, although this route of transmission is much less common.

Nonsexual Transmission of STDs

Nonsexual transmission of STDs is not a contradiction: Because many of the germs that cause STDs thrive in semen, blood, and saliva, nonsexual exposure to one of these fluids can be sufficient to transmit an STD. A person does not need to be sexually mature or sexually active to acquire one of these diseases; even babies can contract an STD, as disease organisms in an infected mother's blood or breast milk can be transferred to her child during pregnancy, childbirth, or nursing.

Transmission of STDs is even possible without direct contact with an infected person. Indeed, it is possible for an infected person to transmit an STD to someone else without ever meeting them. For example, the use of unsterilized dental or medical instruments has been known to mediate the transfer of infected blood and saliva from one patient to another. This method of infection is rare in developed countries such as the United States, but occurs more frequently in poor countries where shortages of medical supplies are common and sterilization procedures are not strictly followed. More well known is transmission of STDs through infected blood in the course of a blood transfusion.

The most common method of nonsexual transmission of STDs in developed countries is by intravenous (IV) injection of drugs, such as heroin, as small amounts of blood are transferred between infected individuals and others who might subsequently share the same needle. The danger of sharing needles is illustrated by the fact that in 1999 half of the Americans who were infected with HIV (the virus that causes the deadly sexually transmitted disease AIDS) were exposed to the virus through IV drug use.

The manner in which an STD is acquired makes no difference in the way it can then be spread. Thus STDs that are contracted nonsexually can be spread both nonsexually and through sexual contact, just as someone who becomes infected with an STD through sexual activity can pass on the disease to someone else sexually and nonsexually.

Significantly, because each STD is caused by a different organism, it is quite possible to contract more than one STD at a time. In fact, research has shown that the presence of some STDs increases

Drug users who share needles are very vulnerable to STDs. Needles contaminated with infected blood can transmit disease.

a person's susceptibility to other STD infections. The U.S. Centers for Disease Control and Prevention (CDC) estimates, for example, that a person already infected with one STD is three to five times more likely to acquire HIV if exposed to the virus than a non-infected person who is exposed to HIV.

STDs Are Not Spread by Casual Contact

Though STDs can be spread nonsexually, the nonsexual transmission of these diseases is almost always limited to direct and immediate contact with infected body fluids. This is because the infectious organisms that cause STDs cannot survive for extended periods outside a living person. Once these organisms are removed from their normal habitat within the body and exposed to the air,

The skin offers protection against casual transmission of most STDs. The parasites that cause scabies (pictured), however, can infect humans through casual contact with the skin.

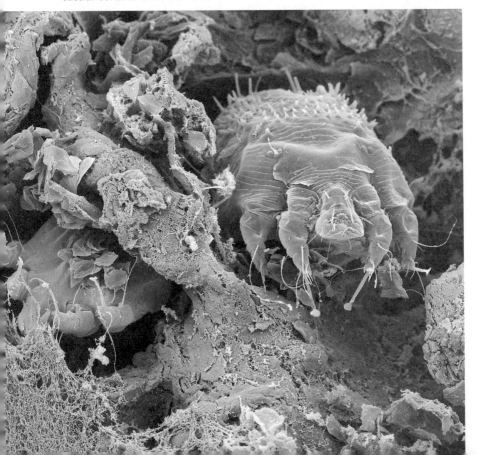

they quickly perish. This means that it is nearly impossible to contract an STD through day-to-day casual interactions such as handshakes, hugs, or the use of public toilet seats, since any disease organisms that are deposited at these external contact points soon die. Even in the rare instance where live organisms are transferred by casual contact, they cannot cause disease unless they penetrate the surface of the skin or come in contact with mucous membranes.

For the most part, skin offers sufficient protection against casual transmission of STDs. Exceptions to this rule are found in the case of two STDs, pubic lice and scabies. The tiny insects that cause these diseases are hardy enough to survive for days on bedding, clothing, or furniture. Thus direct contact between a person's skin and one of these contaminated surfaces can be sufficient to acquire these STDs. However, transmission by this route is very rare. Most people acquire pubic lice and scabies through sexual activity.

STDs Are Common and on the Rise

The fact that sexual activity is a fundamental, or innate, human behavior ensures that STDs occur everywhere among the human population. STDs are among the most common infectious diseases worldwide, with over 350 million new cases occurring across the globe each year. Fifteen million of these new cases occur in the United States alone, a rate of new infection higher than that of any other country in the industrialized world. Indeed, the CDC, the federal agency that monitors the incidence of disease and charts outbreaks, notes that in 1995 five of the ten most frequently reported diseases in the United States—chlamydia, gonorrhea, AIDS, primary and secondary syphilis, and hepatitis B—were STDs, accounting for 87 percent of the total reported cases of these ten diseases. The World Health Organization (WHO) estimates that over 70 million Americans are infected with at least one STD.

Clearly, some STDs are more common than others. In the United States each year, 5.5 million people become infected with a viral STD known as the human papillomavirus (HPV), cited by many as the most common STD. According to an NBC news report, "Some experts estimate that as many as 75% of reproductive age Americans may have been infected with the virus [HPV], which

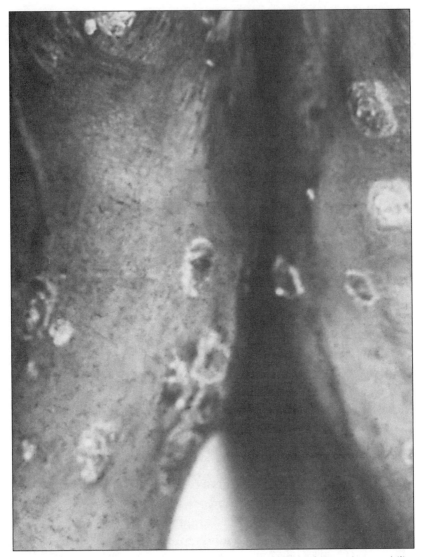

This patient's legs exhibit psoriaform lesions, a symptom of secondary syphilis. Syphilis is one of the more common STDs in the United States.

sometimes disappears within months and sometimes hangs on for years."[1] The parasitic STD trichomoniasis is also extremely common, with over 5 million Americans contracting this disease each year. The STD spreading at the fastest rate, the bacterial infection called chlamydia, currently infects approximately 3 million people annually, and a million Americans acquire genital herpes each year. The relatively few (forty thousand) new cases of HIV infection in the United States does not indicate that the incidence of HIV is diminishing; a January 2003 report by the Association of American Colleges estimates that worldwide more than 5 million people were infected with HIV in 2002 alone.

Recent surveys conducted by a number of health organizations, including CDC and WHO, show that both common and uncommon STDs are on the rise. New cases of chlamydia, HPV, and genital herpes are rising at exponential rates. New cases of genital herpes, for example, have increased by 30 percent in the past twenty years; 45 million Americans, close to one in five over the age of twelve, are infected with this viral STD. Even some STDs whose incidence declined sharply with the introduction of antibiotics have recently seen an upswing. New cases of syphilis, for instance, which were reported at a relatively low and stable level of about one thousand per year in the United States, shot up to more than six thousand in 2001. Gonorrhea is another STD that seemed to be well controlled by antibiotics, with cases steadily decreasing over the last few decades. However, from 2000 to 2002 the incidence of gonorrhea infection in the United States jumped by 9 percent.

HIV infection rates, which steadied and even fell as much as 47 percent in the mid-1990s with increased public awareness of AIDS, have skyrocketed since 1999. That year forty thousand new HIV cases were diagnosed in the United States; though U.S. incidence has remained about the same since then, the HIV epidemic is rising particularly sharply in Eastern Europe and Central Asia, with new cases rising 25 to 30 percent per year in China.

Factors in the Spread of STDs

The acceleration in the incidence of STDs can be attributed to several recent developments in modern societies. The booming world population has been one contributing factor. As population grows and cities become more crowded, contact between people increases and the incidence of STDs increases too. Modern populations are also more mobile than people in the past. Thanks to the widespread construction of roads and train lines, people are now able to routinely move from place to place, transmitting STDs and other diseases wherever they go. Air travel has increased the spread of STDs immeasurably by transporting infected people from one side of the globe to the other in a matter of hours.

The fact that certain STDs can be spread by contaminated blood is another factor in their rising incidence, since medical blood transfusion is a much more common procedure in today's society than it ever was in the past. In the 1980s, before HIV was identified as the cause of AIDS and screening tests were developed to detect HIV in the blood supply, many people were unknowingly infected with HIV-contaminated blood received during blood transfusions.

Sexual attitudes and behaviors have also changed since the invention of the birth control pill in the late 1950s made pregnancy a much less likely result of sexual relations and helped to launch the so-called sexual revolution of the 1960s. For the first time sexual relations were promoted as healthy, pleasurable activities free of the life-long commitment of monogamy or child rearing. As a result, more people tended to have a greater number of sexual partners, which increased the likehood that an infected person would transmit an STD.

According to public health officials, people are not only engaging in sexual relations with a greater number of partners but also are less likely to take precautions to prevent the spread of STDs. Helen Gayle, the director of the CDC's National Center for HIV, STD, and TB Prevention attributes this indifference to the medical successes of the past few decades, when some STDs declined to all-time lows. Gayle says that the recent increase in the incidence of many STDs "should serve as a wake-up call to all people at risk that high-risk sexual behaviors continue to have very real consequences."[2]

The effect of recent developments has been further amplified by the fact that it can take up to several years after STD infection for symptoms of disease to develop. With such a long delay, many, if not most, people transmit an STD before they realize that they have a disease.

Actual Incidence Far Exceeds Reported Cases

Experts estimate that the total number of people infected with STDs is actually much greater than the number of reported cases. For example, the most highly reported STD infection in the United States is chlamydia. In 1999 660,000 cases of chlamydia were recorded in

Sexually transmitted diseases are most common in large, densely populated cities, where infection can rapidly spread.

the United States. The CDC estimates the actual number of cases, however, is approximately 3 million.

One reason for this discrepancy is that in the absence of symptoms many infected people do not know they have a disease and do not seek treatment. Also, a diagnosis of a sexually transmitted disease has traditionally carried a social stigma, and many health care providers choose not to record or report an STD diagnosis to protect their patients' privacy. Connie, a social worker in a San Francisco STD clinic, says that her patients are very concerned that their positive diagnosis is kept confidential. As Connie explains, "There are still a lot of negative connotations associated with having an STD. Nice people aren't supposed to get them, so patients that I see often worry that they will be viewed as sexually promiscuous if anyone were to find out."[3]

Indeed, some people are so embarrassed by the prospect of having an STD that they avoid treatment even when symptoms are obvious. This reluctance is often intensified if the infected person is young and still living in the family home. As Connie explains:

> It isn't as if they have a broken arm or a flu. They'd go to their parents or the school nurse in a second to seek help for those types of problems. . . . Most teens are rather horrified at the idea of discussing any sexual health problem with their parents. For one thing, it would mean admitting that they are sexually active. . . . It often isn't until they feel a significant amount of pain or are seeing mucus in their urine, that they come in here for help.[4]

Although worsening symptoms may force many infected individuals to eventually seek treatment, other people with only mild or no symptoms may remain untreated and risk infecting others.

Who Is Affected by STDs?

Any sexually active person anywhere is at risk of contracting an STD. STDs affect people of all racial, ethnic, cultural, social, economic, and religious groups. To a lesser degree, people of any age, sexually active or not, can contract an STD nonsexually via contaminated body fluids.

However, some groups and activities carry higher risk than others. The majority of new cases occur in people ages fifteen to

Because teenagers are prone to such high-risk behavior as having unprotected sex with multiple partners, they are very vulnerable to STDs.

twenty-five years. Teenagers are one of the highest-risk groups for contracting STDs, with over one quarter of new cases occurring in people under the age of twenty. According to the CDC, this is because teens are more likely than other age group to have multiple partners and to engage in unprotected sex, two high-risk behaviors. Indeed, 45 percent of fifteen- to seventeen-year-olds participating in a Henry J. Kaiser Family Foundation, MTV, and *Teen People* magazine survey reported having three or more sexual partners, and only 57 percent said they used a condom every time they had sex.

This high-risk behavior is resulting in an enormous number of preventable infections. The rates of infection by chlamydia, genital herpes, HPV, gonorrhea, and HIV are higher among teens than among any other age group. Forty percent of all new cases of chlamydia are diagnosed in people under twenty years of age: Among sexually active teens, more than one in ten females and one in twenty males are infected with this disease. Genital herpes is also rampant among the teen population with the highest rates of infection occurring among Caucasian teenagers; at current rates of infection, 15 to 20 percent of teens will be infected with genital herpes by the time they reach adulthood.

People under twenty-five years old also have the highest risk of contracting HIV. Roughly 50 percent of all new cases of HIV are diagnosed in people younger than twenty-five with the fastest-growing incidence among heterosexual females thirteen to nineteen years of age. Thus HIV infection is clearly not limited to the high-risk behaviors with which it is closely associated, primarily IV drug use and unprotected anal sex.

Young Females at Greatest Risk

Although young people of both sexes are at high risk for acquiring STDs, females have an even greater likelihood of infection than males. In addition to the increased rates of chlamydia and HIV in female teens compared to their male peers, the rates of HPV are also highest in young women. Screens for HPV infection have consistently identified this STD in 28 to 46 percent of women twenty-five years of age or younger. Gonorrhea also hits the young female population hardest, with the fifteen- to nineteen-year-old group acquiring the greatest number of infections.

"STDs are inherently sexist," says H. Hunter Handsfield, director of Seattle and King County's STD control program. "They are transmitted more efficiently from male to female than vice versa."[5] This is because the delicate mucosal tissue in the vagina is extremely susceptible to small tears and abrasions which permit infection by STDs. For example, the chance that a female will contract gonorrhea from one act of intercourse with an infected male may be as high as 90 percent, whereas the risk of transmission to a male from an infected female falls to 20 to 30 percent. Similarly, the transfer of HIV infection has been estimated to be eight times higher from male to female than the reverse. Research has also shown that the cervical tissue (connecting the vagina and uterus) of females under twenty years of age is even more sus-

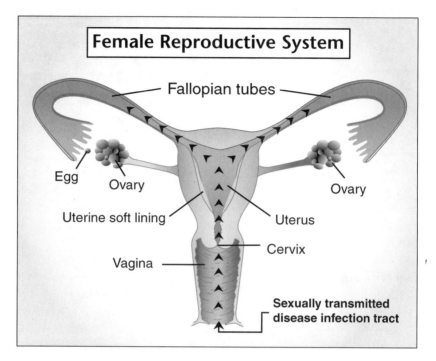

Female Reproductive System

Fallopian tubes

Egg

Ovary

Ovary

Uterine soft lining

Uterus

Cervix

Vagina

Sexually transmitted disease infection tract

ceptible to infection by chlamydia and gonorrhea than that of older females.

Dating habits and social patterns also influence the suscepti-bility of females to STDs. For example, hetrosexual females often become sexually involved with males who are older than them-selves. Older partners are more likely to have been sexually active longer with more partners and are therefore more likely to be in-fected with an STD than younger males.

The Effects of STDs

STDs have a wide range of medical, economic, and social effects, depending on specific disease and treatment options, but collec-tively it is clear that STDs exact a huge toll on humanity. The most immediate effect is the acute symptoms of disease an infected in-dividual suffers, including pain and discomfort that disrupts a per-son's personal habits, sexual activity, and ability to work for days or weeks despite effective treatment.

Although some STDs can be cured, many lead to chronic health problems such as repeated outbreaks and chronic inflammation

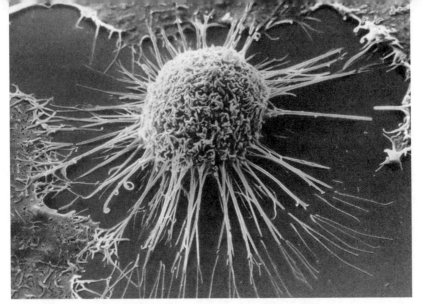

One serious complication for women infected with HIV is cervical cancer. Shown here is a micrograph of a cancer cell.

that is potentially disabling and disfiguring. Of increasing concern to health care providers and public health agencies are the long-term effects of STDs, which can cause a wide range of other diseases from chronic hepatitis to cancer.

The long-term complications of STDs are well recognized in females, in whom the symptoms of STDs such as gonorrhea, syphilis, and chlamydia are masked and take longer to develop. Females thus remain infected for longer periods of time before seeking treatment. This delay in treatment can give the infection time to spread to the internal reproductive organs resulting in the development of pelvic inflammatory disease (PID). PID is a leading cause of chronic pelvic pain, internal abscess formation, and infertility in women. Over one million women in the United States experience an acute episode of PID each year with one hundred thousand becoming infertile as a result. In addition, PID causes a large proportion of ectopic pregnancies, a potentially life-threatening condition in which a fertilized egg fails to descend into the uterus. Continued development of the egg in the fallopian tube can result in rupture of the tube and death of the pregnant woman.

HPV infection causes serious complications in females; HPV is linked to more than half the cases of cervical cancer in American women. Approximately 12,800 cases of cervical cancer were diagnosed in the United States in 2000, and close to 4,600 women died of the disease in 2001.

STD infection in pregnant women can also have devastating consequences for the baby, both during and after pregnancy. A high number of spontaneous abortions, stillbirths, and premature deliveries are caused by STD infections. Syphilis is particularly dangerous in pregnant women, killing up to 40 percent of unborn fetuses. STDs can also cause brain damage, blindness, disfigurement, and chronic respiratory distress in children born to infected mothers. In addition, the STD itself may be transmitted, with the child exhibiting the same symptoms as the infected mother. Among the most serious infections that can be spread from mother to child is HIV, since the child will then develop AIDS. The risk of HIV transfer from mother to child may be as high as 25 percent and

A young woman holds her baby at a hospital in Bucharest, Romania. Because the mother is infected with HIV, her child will almost certainly develop AIDS.

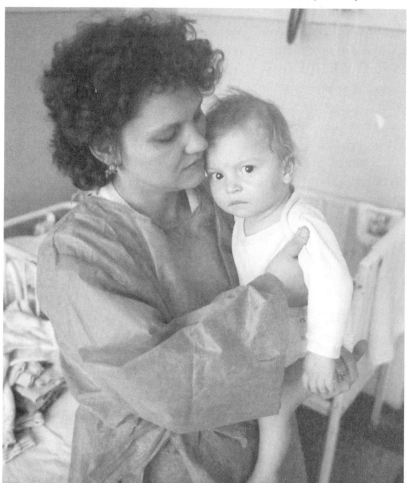

usually occurs during birth. However, HIV can be transmitted during pregnancy and even afterward, with 10 to 15 percent of mother-child transmission occurring through breast milk.

The most serious long-term effects of STDs are associated with AIDS, the most intensely researched and most dangerous STD because it is incurable and fatal. The scope and scale of the AIDS epidemic is unprecedented: More than 65 million people worldwide have been infected with HIV since the epidemic began in the 1970s, 25 million of whom have died as of January 2003. AIDS is the fourth-leading cause of death worldwide and the leading cause of death in Africa, reducing average life expectancy on the African continent from sixty-two to forty-seven years and severely destabilizing African society.

From an economic perspective, the consequences of STDs are enormous. The yearly cost of treating STDs in the United States alone exceeds $10 billion, a figure that does not include the indirect but substantial costs associated with loss in work productivity and attempts to overcome infertility caused by STDs. Direct treatment of HPV costs $1.6 billion annually. It is difficult to estimate the worldwide financial cost of HIV/AIDS, but a 2003 Association of American Colleges and Universities briefing suggests that an annual international investment of between $8.7 billion and $12 billion in HIV/AIDS care, services, and prevention is required.

Clearly STDs have calamitous effects on humankind. Given the significant medical, financial, and social costs of STDs, controlling their spread is essential. The first step in combating STDs is accurate diagnosis and prompt treatment.

Chapter 2

Diagnosis and Treatment of STDs

THERE ARE MORE than twenty different organisms that can infect humans through sexual activity resulting in disease. Because STDs can arise from such a wide array of infectious organisms and because different STDs can produce similar symptoms, or no symptoms, diagnosis and treatment of STDs can be difficult. Precise diagnosis is essential, however, for two reasons: Sexually transmitted diseases do not go away by themselves, and successfully treating an STD depends on prescribing the correct drug or therapy for each disease.

The Importance of Early Detection

No matter which STD an individual is infected with, the time between initial infection and treatment is an important factor in the outcome of the disease. STDs that are treated soon after they are acquired have the best prognosis since there is less chance that the infection will spread to other parts of the body and develop into a more serious condition. Also, finding out about an STD sooner rather than later helps to curtail its spread, since STDs can be eliminated through treatment or the infected person can take precautions to prevent transmission.

Early diagnosis is more likely when symptoms of an STD are immediate, painful, and too alarming to be ignored. Tom, who was fifteen when he acquired an STD that produced symptoms quickly, did not wait long before visiting his doctor. Tom says, "The burning sensation that I felt [when urinating] was so intense that I couldn't stand it anymore."[6] Common symptoms such as discharge from the vagina or penis; the appearance of blisters or sores on the genitals; and pain, itching, or burning sensations during urination or sexual intercourse may arise within days of acquiring an STD. As in Tom's case, the onset of symptoms such as these is a clear indication that something is wrong, and the location of the infection is obvious to both the sufferer and the physician. Not surprisingly, these kinds of STDs are the easiest to diagnose.

Unfortunately, many people do not receive treatment in a timely manner because some STDs do not produce obvious symptoms; an infected person simply does not know that he or she is infected. The initial symptoms of an STD may be too subtle to notice or similar to the mild symptoms of other common illnesses, and may not be related to the genitals. HIV infection, for example, initially causes only mild flulike symptoms that go away within a few days; other STDs may cause rashes or sores on the arms or torso that an infected person might mistake for an allergic reaction or insect bite.

One of the most problematic aspects of STDs, and a major reason why many people do not seek prompt medical treatment, is that the majority of STDs remain completely silent for months and often years before triggering symptoms. Nevertheless, throughout the asymptomatic stages the infection may be progressing and damaging the body. This lag in the development of symptoms is obviously detrimental to preventing the spread of STDs, as many people will transmit the disease before they are aware of the infection. Felicia Stewart, a reproductive-health expert with the health maintenance organization Kaiser Permanente, cites the asymptomatic nature of STDs as a major reason why they are so easily transmitted. Felicia says, "There's no way to know if you have an STD without getting tested. Even the doctors don't know."[7]

STD Testing Sites

Although the signs of STD infection may not be apparent, all STDs can be accurately diagnosed with medical assistance and testing. This means that they can be detected and treated during the earliest stages of infection, before the most serious damage occurs. For this reason health care professionals recommend that all sexually active people be screened for STD infections once a year, or

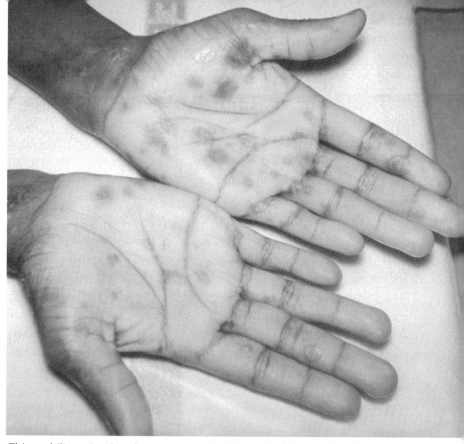

This syphilis patient's palms are covered with rough skin eruptions that also appear on the soles of the feet.

more frequently if they have had more than one sexual partner during that time. An immediate medical checkup is warranted if a current or past sexual partner is diagnosed with an STD, since the risk that the disease has been transmitted is high. Diagnosing an STD early on is preferable to letting the infection progress; however, taking steps to avoid becoming infected in the first place is better still. Therefore the best time to be screened for an STD is before initiating a new sexual relationship. If prospective partners are tested and treated for STDs prior to engaging in sexual activity with each other, the risk of transmitting an STD can be virtually eliminated.

Once a person decides to be tested for STDs, the next step is to find a place to perform the tests and diagnosis. The range of choices in most communities is wide. Most family practice or internal medicine physicians in private practice can perform STD testing in their offices. Most cities sponsor public health clinics that specialize in

STD screening along with prenatal care or immunizations. The choice between a private doctor's office and a clinic is usually influenced by cost, privacy, and convenience. Many public clinics are free and offer anonymous testing; instead of creating a medical record naming the patient, as most private physicians do, these clinics use only a number to associate patients with their STD test results. On the other hand, the service provided by a private doctor is often more personalized and may be closer to home. Some people are more comfortable discussing an STD with a doctor with whom they have a long history; others find it embarrassing to broach the topic with their family doctor. Both private doctors and STD clinics are medically competent to diagnose and treat these diseases; patients are advised to choose the facility where they will be most comfortable, most free to ask questions, and most receptive to advice.

The STD Testing Procedure

Regardless of where a person goes to be tested for an STD, the testing process is similar. Patients are asked to provide their medical history and specific information about their sexual activity, safe-sex practices, and symptoms. Responses to these questions help the health care professional to determine which STDs the patient should be tested for. Although a description of the symptoms that the patient is experiencing can assist the health care professional in making a diagnosis, it is rarely sufficient. Different STDs can exhibit similar symptoms and a single type of STD can manifest itself in remarkably different ways depending on the individual.

Blood, urine, or specimens from areas of the body that are likely to be infected are usually collected from the patient for analysis by a clinical laboratory, which may take up to two or three weeks. In addition, a physical examination is conducted to check for visible signs of STD infection. The precise areas of the body that are examined depends on the patient's sex and the likelihood that the patient has been exposed to particular STDs. At some stage of the visit, patients are usually given the opportunity to discuss any concerns they may have about STDs with the health care professional. In addition to answering questions about disease progression and treatment, the health care professional can provide valuable information about the prevention of STDs. Clinics that specialize in STD screening usually offer pamphlets on a range of related topics, which can also be helpful to the patient. After the examination, patients are told how they can find out the results of the tests. Sometimes the patient can access the results by telephone or mail, with the understanding that a follow-up appointment will be necessary to begin treatment if a positive diagnosis is made.

Diagnosing STDs means differentiating between four main categories of infectious agents. A few STDs are caused by tiny insects that can be seen with the naked eye. The majority of STDs, however, are caused by germs that are too small to be seen without the aid of a microscope. In general the germs responsible for STDs fall into the classes of protozoa, bacteria, or viruses.

Diagnosing and Treating Curable STDs

STDs caused by insects can be easily cured. Among all curable STDs, pubic lice and scabies are the easiest to diagnose because the

Pubic lice look like little crabs under a microscope. Pubic lice and scabies are among the most easily treated STDs.

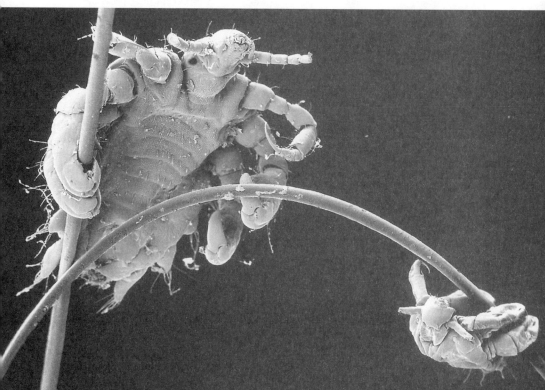

characteristic symptom of intense itching at the site of infection is nearly unmistakable and the infecting insects can be seen on close visual examination. Adult pubic lice, also known as *Pthirus pubis*, look like little crabs about one millimeter in length. *Sarcoptes scabiei*, the mites that cause scabies, are about the same size as pubic lice but resemble a tiny tick. Because these insects can be seen without a microscope, laboratory tests are not required for a health care professional to make a definitive diagnosis. Both pubic lice and scabies can be cured by the application of prescriptive lotions or shampoos that contain chemical ingredients that kill these insects. How-

Trichomonas vaginalis, *one of the largest STD germs, can easily be detected and treated with oral antibiotics.*

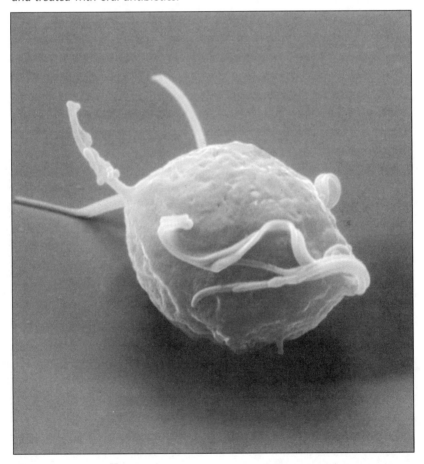

ever, the ability of these insects to survive for extended periods of time without human contact means that reinfestation is possible. In order to eliminate all possible sources of reinfestation, all clothing and furniture that have been in contact with the infected person must be treated or laundered with special chemical agents. Alternatively, washable items can be laundered in very hot water (125 degrees Fahrenheit), dried at a high temperature, and ironed at high heat.

Unlike pubic lice and scabies, most STDs cannot be diagnosed simply by looking for the infecting organism with the naked eye. The identification of organisms that are microscopic in size is necessarily more complex and relies on the use of specialized technology. Many of the infecting germs are large enough to be seen with a standard laboratory microscope and sometimes visual identification is all that is required to diagnose the disease. This is the case for the protozoan STD trichomoniasis, a disease that primarily strikes females and causes pain and vaginal discharge. Because the infecting protozoan, *Trichomonas vaginalis,* is one of the largest STD germs and is distinctively shaped like a tiny oval jellyfish, it can be easily diagnosed by microscopic examination of a vaginal swab. Treatment of trichomoniasis is also quite simple, requiring only oral antibiotics to cure the infection.

Several STDs caused by bacteria can also be easily visualized under the microscope. However, because many bacteria are of similar shape and size, visualization of these germs is not always helpful in diagnosing a specific STD. Conclusive diagnosis requires that the bacteria from an infected person be cultured in the laboratory so that additional tests can be performed. To accomplish this, samples of the patient's blood, urine, or specimens from other likely sites of infection are added to several types of bacterial growth media and incubated at body temperature for several days. If a sufficient quantity of the bacteria can be cultured, a variety of biochemical tests are conducted in order to precisely identify the bacteria.

One advantage of this type of diagnosis is that fluid samples can be taken even in the absence of an active, or symptomatic, outbreak, detecting infection even during a "silent" stage. It is not always successful, however, due to the difficulty of growing bacteria in culture. Ways to get around this problem have been recently devised to distinguish between certain bacterial STDs based on their unique genetic content. Because this type of analysis requires only a small quantity of bacteria, the amount of bacteria contained within the patient's original sample is sufficient and growth of the bacteria is not necessary.

Once the bacteria has been identified, treatment is relatively straightforward. All STDs of bacterial origin can be treated with antibiotics, although the specific kind of antibiotic prescribed will depend on the type of bacteria that is causing the disease. For chlamydia, gonorrhea, and bacterial vaginosis, oral antibiotics are sufficient to completely cure the disease. A more aggressive treatment consisting of injectable antibiotics is required to cure the bacterial STDs syphilis and chancroid.

Diagnosis and Treatment of Incurable STDs

In comparison with other STDs, the treatment options available for people infected with genital warts, herpes, hepatitis B, and AIDS

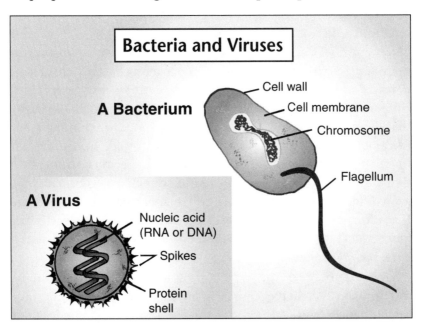

Bacteria and Viruses

A Bacterium

Cell wall
Cell membrane
Chromosome
Flagellum

A Virus

Nucleic acid
(RNA or DNA)
Spikes
Protein
shell

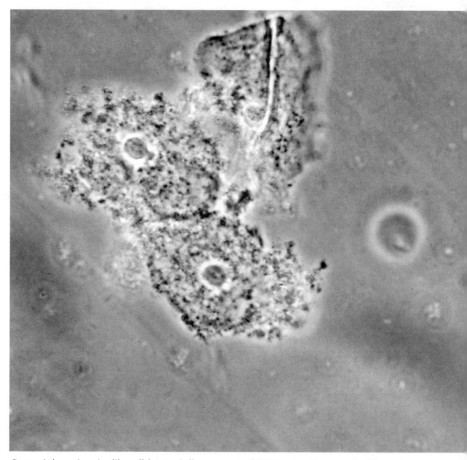

Bacterial vaginosis, like all bacterially generated STDs, can be cured with oral antibiotics.

are not very effective. All of these STDs are caused by a type of germ known as a virus. Unlike most bacteria and protozoa, viruses actually enter the cells of their host organism and destroy them from within, spending a significant amount of their life cycle inside the cells that they infect. This makes it difficult to kill virus particles without also killing the cells of the infected person and risking the person's life. For this reason most viral STDs cannot be cured.

Viruses are by far the smallest of the organisms that cause STDs. They are typically one hundred times smaller than most bacteria, so tiny that approximately 50 billion viruses could fit as a single layer on a two-by-two-inch postage stamp. The miniscule size of viruses means that they cannot be visualized using a conventional microscope. Sometimes viral STDs are diagnosed based on the distinctive physical symptoms they produce, sometimes by detecting the distinctive antibodies to the virus that the body produces in response to infection. These are indirect methods of diagnosis. It is possible to directly identify the presence of the virus itself, but this requires sophisticated techniques that are available only at specialized laboratories. These techniques produce a "molecular picture" of a virus's external features or genetic identity. In this manner, fast and reliable data is generated for the detection and identification of viruses that are present within blood samples or other specimens.

Though advanced techniques for diagnosis of viral STDs are now available, the development of effective treatment has a long way to go. The best existing treatments may reduce the symptoms or the spread of some viral STDs, but they usually fall short of a complete cure. Often people infected with a viral STD will experience recurring symptoms that appear and disappear in an unpredictable manner. In genital herpes, caused by a virus related to the chickenpox and cold-sore viruses, these recurring symptoms consist of outbreaks of painful blistering sores on or around the genitals or mouth. According to one herpes patient, "The physical pain was terrible. Walking, sitting and going to the bathroom hurt so bad, I had to bite on a towel to stand the pain. If you've ever had canker sores in your mouth, imagine having 20 of them in an even more sensitive area."[8] Treatment for herpes consists of oral and topical medications that inhibit viral replication, thereby decreasing the frequency and occurrence of outbreaks and reducing the chance of transmission to sexual partners. Despite these benefits, the treatments are rarely successful in alleviating all symptoms and do not provide a cure for the virus, so the infection remains for life.

Infection by HPV is also lifelong. This virus results in the development of warts on or within the genitals. Although genital warts are rarely painful, they can be unsightly and contagious and may cause problems during urination, intercourse, or childbirth. The treatment of genital warts is relatively time-consuming, requiring repeated visits to the doctor or clinic to remove the warts by cryosurgery, or freezing. Because this treatment does not eliminate the infecting virus, the warts can grow back after they are removed. Even when the warts are gone, a person may still be contagious. Michele, a twenty-four-year-old woman who is currently receiving

Genital herpes produces painful, recurring blisters. Although outbreaks can be controlled with drugs, no cure for the disease exists.

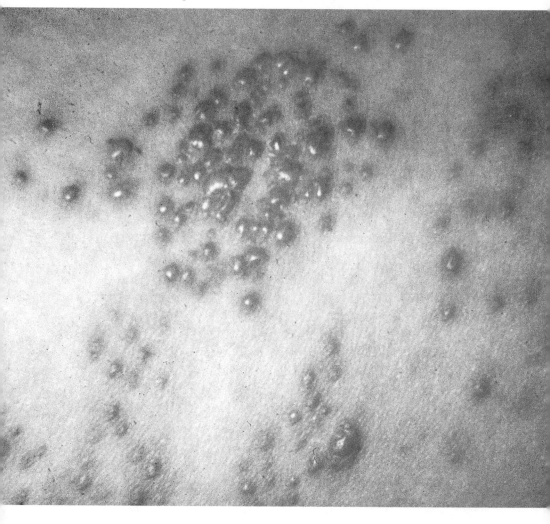

cryotherapy treatment for genital warts, knows the risks only too well. She says, "At first I was mad at my boyfriend for not telling me, but he had his genital warts removed 10 years ago and he didn't think he could spread the virus after having them removed."[9] One of the more insidious aspects of HPV is that it can be transmitted to others even if warts never appear. The fact is that only 1 percent of those infected by HPV develop warts. According to Marshall Glover, director of the National STD Hotline, "The body is really good at keeping this virus in check. Many people also think you can't get a disease like genital warts unless you can see warts on your partner. That's not true."[10] Glover says that the silent nature of HPV explains why transmission rates continue to soar. For females, the consequences of becoming infected with HPV can be much more serious than the potential development of genital warts, as it increases the risk of developing cervical cancer. For this reason, females who are diagnosed with HPV are urged to have an annual Pap smear to detect any signs of cervical cancer as early as possible.

Hepatitis B is unique among STDs in that it rarely requires medical intervention. Although infection by the hepatitis B virus can result in liver function disorders, most of the symptoms are self-limiting and not severe enough to warrant treatment. However, in some cases infection with this virus progresses to cirrhosis, chronic hepatitis, and the development of liver cancer. In these cases, oral drugs will be used to control the disease, but in cases where the disease progresses and becomes life-threatening, the patient may require a liver transplant. For the vast majority of those infected by hepatitis B, the symptoms of infection resolve themselves and the virus remains more or less dormant inside the body.

AIDS, the syndrome caused by the most well-known STD virus, HIV, is a fatal disease in a category of its own. HIV destroys an infected person's immune system, or ability to fight disease, and so treatments focus on the many so-called opportunistic diseases that AIDS patients fall victim to, including pneumonia, cancer, and serious central nervous system infections. Treatment regimens also focus on inhibiting HIV replication within the body, or keeping the

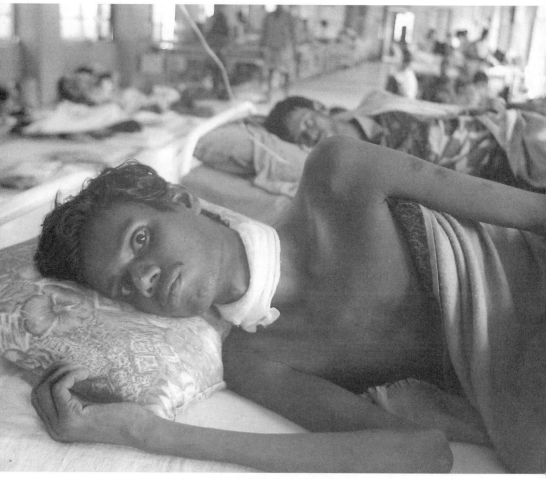

This man is one of nearly four hundred HIV-positive patients in a clinic in India. HIV destroys the immune system, and makes those infected vulnerable to a number of diseases.

virus in check as long as possible, thereby delaying the destruction of the body's essential immune-system cells as long as possible. The sooner treatment begins, the longer an AIDS patient will be able to live and work normally.

STDs Are Unpredictable

Even though most STDs are not life-threatening, early medical intervention for STDs is also important for the simple reason that these diseases are unpredictable. Because in most cases people cannot reliably identify an infected partner and therefore cannot be certain that they themselves are disease-free, the routine screening of everyone who is sexually active is recommended for early detection of disease. Furthermore, because the unique physiology of the infected person affects disease progression, it is often difficult to anticipate the outcome of an STD. STDs such as HPV and hepatitis B may remain asymptomatic in most people but can be life-threatening in others. Regular follow-up by a trained medical professional is indispensable for preserving the health of people with STDs. Careful monitoring of those with asymptomatic STDs allows subtle changes that can be indicative of disease progression to be detected and allows the health care professional to take immediate action to prevent further deterioration. Although the effects of all STDs can be lessened by medical intervention, the deadly and incurable nature of many of these diseases and the complexity and costs of available treatment for STDs lead strongly to the conclusion that prevention is the best strategy for stopping the STD epidemic.

Chapter 3

The Challenge of Prevention

H UMANS HAVE BEEN trying for centuries to rid themselves of STDs, but not one of these diseases is close to worldwide eradication and deadly new ones have appeared in recent years. Effective cures for many STDs, including gonorrhea and chlamydia, have been available for over sixty years, yet outbreaks of these and other STDs continue to take their toll on human health. If cures do not hold the answer for vanquishing STDs, then the solution may need to come from another source, namely prevention.

According to Anthony S. Fauci, the director of the National Institute of Allergy and Infectious Diseases, "There is no more important goal of medical research than to prevent diseases from occurring in the first place."[11] Not only would prevention of STDs alleviate the human misery caused by these diseases, but it would reduce the enormous financial burden incurred by current therapies and the development of new treatments.

Effective, inexpensive methods of STD prevention already exist. The real challenge in preventing STDs lies in getting people to adopt these methods. Making people aware of the dangers of STDs and ways to prevent them is only part of the battle. The success of STD prevention ultimately rests on the ability to instigate changes in sexual attitudes and human behavior, which is not a simple task.

STD-Free—Guaranteed!

The only guaranteed way to prevent sexual transmission of STDs is to abstain from sex altogether. Celibacy, or sexual abstinence, is the most effective way to prevent STDs because it eliminates the primary transmission pathway for these diseases. Nonsexual transmission through contact with contaminated blood is the second most common avenue for STD transmission. However, if a person is not a user of intraveneous drugs, his or her chances of acquiring an STD by this route are close to zero. Clearly, however, though promoting sexual abstinence is a primary prevention strategy aimed at teenagers and young adults, total abstinence is not a realistic or desirable expectation in the long term.

For those who are sexually active, limiting the number of sexual partners is the next best way to reduce the chances of con-

Teens from the Pure Love Alliance march in Philadelphia to promote sexual abstinence and fidelity as ways to prevent STDs.

tracting an STD. The optimal situation is a monogamous relationship between two people who are sexually active only with each other. Even in monogamous relationships, however, there is still a tangible risk of STD transmission if either person has had previous sexual partners. Connie, a social worker at an STD clinic, says, "You can't evaluate the chances of getting an STD from a person whose sexual history is unknown to you. I know its been said many times before, but when you have sex with someone, you aren't just [having sex] with them, you are also [having sex] with all of their previous sexual partners."[12] For this reason, people who are initiating a sexual relationship should undergo a medical examination to check for the presence of STDs before having sex with each other. If both partners undergo testing and complete treatments for them, if any are required, the risk of passing an STD to each other is greatly diminished.

A more aggressive approach to ensuring that people who are sexually active are STD-free is to perform periodic testing for these diseases. Given that many STDs are spread by people who do not realize that they are infected, testing people for infection and treating those who are found to have STDs can greatly help to decrease the overall incidence of these diseases. Due to cost and limited resources it is not feasible to screen everyone. For this reason, all STD-screening programs to date have focused on groups that have a high risk of infection, including youths, commercial-sex workers, some immigrant groups, and health care workers who come in contact with blood products. Some STDs are more appropriate for this strategy than others. Syphilis, in particular, is being targeted through screening programs because the overall incidence of this disease is at an all-time low and most current cases are confined to specific cities or regions of the country. In contrast, screening for STDs like chlamydia, which have a high incidence and are spread over a wide geographic area, require such a large investment in time and money that other methods of prevention may be more effective.

Screening tests alone, however, do not serve to fully inform both partners in a sexual relationship about their mutual STD status. Test results are released only to the patient, who must then broach the subject of positive results with the partner. This sensitive discussion can be difficult in either new or established relationships; embarrassment or fear of rejection can cause people to alter or hide information from a sexual partner. So, from a practical standpoint, it is not always prudent to assume that a sexual partner is free of infection and will remain so for the duration of the relationship. In many situations, additional precautions need to be taken to prevent the transmission of STDs.

Condoms: Good but Not Fail-Safe

One way to prevent the transmission of most STDs between sexual partners is to use a latex condom. This protective device, which is inexpensive and readily available from drugstores and supermarkets, lowers the chance of STD transmission by preventing direct contact between body tissues and bodily fluids, such as sperm, most likely to be infected. Most condoms work by covering the penis with a thin, snug layer of latex. Although male condoms from non-latex materials are available and work well for preventing pregnancy, they do not provide an effective barrier for tiny organisms, such as HIV. Female condoms that are placed within the vagina are also available, although slightly more expensive than those for men.

There is good evidence to show that the use of latex condoms can make a difference in the transmission of many STDs. A study in Europe that looked at the impact of condom use on HIV transmission between couples showed that 123 people remained negative for the virus despite the HIV-positive status of their partners. Other studies have found a strong correlation between the increase in condom use that began in the late 1980s, prompted by fear of AIDS, and the sharp drop that was seen in the incidence of all STDs until the late 1990s. One of the greatest success stories is a national program to decrease HIV transmission, initiated by the Thai government in 1991. Whereas condoms were used in only 25 percent of commercial sex acts in Thailand in 1989, this proportion rose to 94 percent in 1995, halving the transmission of HIV and resulting in a dramatic decrease in new cases of curable STDs.

Encouraging as this seems, the protection afforded by a condom is only as reliable as the person using it. In order to be effective in

A billboard in Bangkok, Thailand, encourages the use of condoms to prevent the spread of AIDS.

preventing STD transmission, a condom must be worn correctly and must be used for every act of intercourse. And even when condoms are used correctly and consistently, they are not 100 percent fail-safe. Condoms can slip and tear occasionally during intercourse, permitting contact and fluid transmission, and condoms cannot always adequately cover an infected region such as a herpes breakout.

Vaccines and Preventive Drugs

The protection afforded by condoms is not complete, so researchers have turned to the development of vaccines against STDs, which offer several advantages. In many ways, vaccines are an ideal form of protection against STDs since they do not require a voluntary

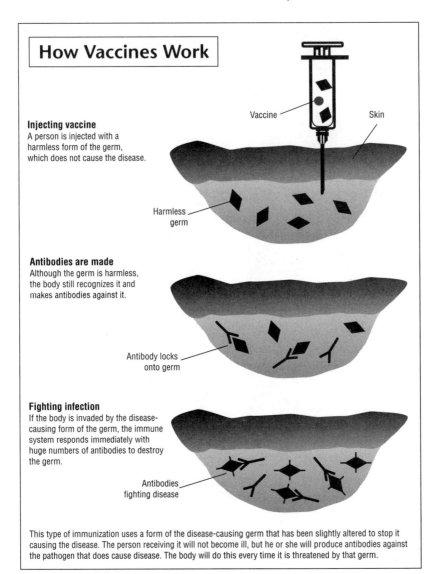

How Vaccines Work

Injecting vaccine
A person is injected with a harmless form of the germ, which does not cause the disease.

Vaccine

Skin

Harmless germ

Antibodies are made
Although the germ is harmless, the body still recognizes it and makes antibodies against it.

Antibody locks onto germ

Fighting infection
If the body is invaded by the disease-causing form of the germ, the immune system responds immediately with huge numbers of antibodies to destroy the germ.

Antibodies fighting disease

This type of immunization uses a form of the disease-causing germ that has been slightly altered to stop it causing the disease. The person receiving it will not become ill, but he or she will produce antibodies against the pathogen that does cause disease. The body will do this every time it is threatened by that germ.

change in behavior or sexual practices and their effects are long lasting. All that is required is a simple injection that contains a non-infectious form of the disease organism. The introduction of this harmless variant into the body allows the immune system to prepare defenses against the particular germ, so that the real germ can be successfully fought off if it is encountered years or even decades in the future.

Although vaccines have been developed and proven effective against many dangerous epidemic diseases such as smallpox and polio, the only successful vaccine against STDs is that developed for hepatitis B. The hepatitis B vaccine is now offered among other standard childhood immunizations and gives close to 100 percent protection against the disease. The vaccine may also be given to adults and is strongly recommended for sexually active adolescents, health care workers, homosexual men, and people whose sexual partners are infected with the virus.

Successful vaccines against other STDs are not yet available. However, recent breakthroughs have been made in preventing the transmission of HIV using new antiviral drugs. These drugs reduce the number of viral particles in the bloodstream to undetectable levels. This not only substantially increases the life span of people who are already infected with HIV but also reduces the chance of transmission of HIV to others during sexual activity and from infected pregnant women to their babies because so few viral particles are present. Some evidence even suggests that immediate dosage of antiviral drugs following initial exposure to HIV can perhaps prevent HIV infection from taking hold. Because such potent antiviral drugs have serious side effects, however, they are not suitable for widespread prescription to healthy people as a prevention measure.

Prevention Requires Changing Behavior

No matter what prevention strategy is adopted, all require the individual to take voluntary, responsible action. Regardless of whether the action involves the purchase and use of condoms, submitting to screening tests, taking medications or getting vaccinated, or abstaining from sex altogether, remaining STD-free is not a passive exercise.

Taking a proactive role in preventing STD transmission is hard simply because changing behavior is hard. Taking individual action is complicated by social, cultural, and even religious barriers that interfere with prevention strategies. For example, some cultures that do not approve of artificial contraception discourage the use of condoms, which prevent pregnancy as well as STDs. Traditional social perceptions that people who use condoms are sexually promiscuous, and therefore held up to criticism or ridicule, are also hard to change. And many people find it all too easy to decide that condoms are a nuisance to use and reduce pleasurable sensation during sex and so choose not to use them.

Major well-funded efforts promoting the use of condoms and other methods of STD prevention have changed anticondom attitudes to some degree, but such programs are somewhat undermined by the powerful influence of the mass media and its popular portrayal of sexual intercourse as an exciting and worry-free activity. According to former U.S. surgeon general David Satcher, "Media programming rarely depicts sexual behavior in the context of a long-term relationship, use of contraceptives, or the po-

Efforts to promote safe sex, such as New York University's condom awareness day, are often undermined by glamorous portrayals of unprotected sex in mass media.

tentially negative consequences of sexual behavior."[13] Despite the media's damaging reinforcement of high-risk sexual behavior, Satcher is quick to note that the media has an equally potent ability to promote safe sexual practices. This is supported by a recent national survey in which teenagers rated magazines and television as among the top five ways that they learned about STDs and ways to prevent them.

Young People Are the Least Likely to Take Precautions Against STDs

Reports about STDs by the media have been particularly prolific since the emergence of HIV/AIDS. This, together with the emergence of the Internet, means that people are experiencing unprecedented access to information about STDs and ways to prevent them. Yet awareness of STDs and safe sexual practices is far from complete, and many people, especially young people, fail to put their knowledge regarding STD protection into practice. A January 2003 briefing by the Association of American Colleges and Universities notes that 50 percent of fifteen- to twenty-four-year-olds in key developing countries in the Caribbean, Central Asia, Eastern Europe, and East Asia have never heard of HIV or AIDS. It comes as no coincidence that this age group has the highest incidence of STDs.

Ignorance is not the only reason young people do not adopt prevention methods. Peer pressure can work against prevention by discouraging instead of promoting abstinence, the only guaranteed method of STD prevention. Katie, seventeen, from Oregon says, "Sooo many people feel like all their friends are doing it and they're left out. It just ends up that no one wants to be the last person to have sex."[14] Many young people cope with this pressure by not talking about their choice to be celibate, while others, like Thom Pasculli, eighteen, are vocal about their decision. Thom says, "Believe it or not, I have no problem admitting that I'm a virgin. I don't need a support group, and I don't care what other people think (although everyone I've told has expressed respect)."[15]

Denial also plays a potent role in the failure of people to protect themselves against these diseases. Young people, in particular, are prone to dismiss the consequences of high-risk activities. According to high school junior Alison Forbes, seventeen, many of her peers are more worried about how sex will affect their relationship than whether it will put them at risk for catching an STD. Alison says, "People don't like to think about [catching STDs]."[16] Heidi Chuckel, who is eighteen years old and a high school senior, says, "They don't consider what could happen. It's not a lack of knowledge; it's a lack of understanding. We know the facts. It's just that people, especially those in their youth, think they are untouchable."[17] A national survey by the Kaiser Family Foundation, MTV, and *Teen People* in 1999 concurs with these opinions showing that only one-fifth of those between fifteen and seventeen years of age believe there is a risk of contracting an STD with a single sexual encounter.

The current increase in unprotected sex among young male homosexuals is another example of rational decisions taking a back seat to impulsive, high-risk behavior. Although educational campaigns within the gay community were highly effective at promoting safe sexual practices early in the AIDS epidemic, many men are now choosing to ignore these messages and engage in high-risk sexual activity. Tim Alderman, who is forty-seven years old and a member of the gay community in Sydney, Australia, says:

> It is interesting to note that there is a current rise in the rate of infections from 'old-fashioned' STD's in the gay community at the moment, especially [gonorrhea]. I feel that HIV has become a 'generational' thing [i.e., a product of my generation], and that the young ones think they are immune. This is the problem with a disease becoming unfashionable—no one takes it seriously anymore. The youngsters on the scene see HIV and the safe-sex lifestyle as something they are immune from. It cropped up in my generation, we suffered all the problems caused by it, we solved a lot of the problems and biases, and now it is in the past. They think it will never happen to them (ah, the innocence of youth); therefore they are no longer practicing safe sex, and think they will never get HIV. Consequently, STD's are back.[18]

Although safe sex campaigns were successful in the early years of the AIDS epidemic, many men now admit to having unprotected sex on a regular basis.

Failure to Communicate Helps to Spread STDs

The tendency to ignore messages about safe sex is accompanied by widespread reluctance between sexual partners to talk about STDs with each other. The national survey by the Kaiser Family Foundation, MTV, and *Teen People* found that talking about STDs, even with friends, was something most people would rather avoid. Over 70 percent of Americans ranked this topic of conversation as anxiety-provoking, and discussion of STDs with a sexual partner was viewed as awkward by nearly 40 percent. Less talk about STDs means less action, in terms of prevention. People are not as informed, less aware, and more likely to contract an STD than they would be if the topic was easily discussed over the dinner table.

While the lack of communication about STDs detracts from promoting the message of safe sex as a whole, the real problem arises when those who have been diagnosed with an STD fail to tell their previous and current sexual partners about their disease. According to Connie, "People think that if they have an STD they will be judged by others as sexually promiscuous and morally loose. The unfortunate result of this attitude is that it can prevent people [diagnosed with an STD] from telling their sexual partners that they should come in and get tested. It really is a huge problem for stopping the spread of these diseases."[19] The Kaiser survey supports that viewpoint in reporting that 82 percent of teenagers say telling a sexual partner about a positive result for an STD test would be uncomfortable and 52 percent say it would be *very* uncomfortable. Although the majority of people in all age groups viewed notification of a sexual partner as an obligation, a sizable minority did not hold this belief. Teenagers in particular indicated that the need to notify a partner that they were infected with an STD infection could be dismissed if condoms were always used or if sexual activity occurred only when no symptoms were apparent.

Official intervention to selectively screen all previous and current sexual partners of people who have been diagnosed with an STD is one way to get around relying on the infected individual to communicate information. It has been argued that diagnosis and treatment of STDs within this high-risk population would be an efficient means to short-circuit the spread of these diseases and would go a long way toward gaining control of the epidemic. This approach is theoretical, however, because several problems make its practical application unlikely. First, it is not always possible to identify all sexual partners of a person who has been diagnosed with an STD. Even when sexual partners can be identified, the obligation of doctors to keep the details of their patient's health confidential prevents notification of partners without the patient's permission. More often than not, the potentially touchy situation of informing sexual partners that they may have contracted an STD is left to the patient. Alerting sexual partners that they may have an STD is only the first step in the process. There is no guarantee that those who are notified will present themselves for testing and treatment. Denial, embarrassment, and a simple reluctance to go to a doctor or clinic for testing can undermine the most persistent attempts to treat the partners of people with STDs. To overcome this hurdle, a pilot project is currently being run in the United States to test the effectiveness of sending positively diagnosed patients home with medication for their sexual partners as well as themselves. It is hoped that this may prevent inertia or embarrassment from being a stumbling block to receiving treatment.

STD Education in Schools: A Controversial Issue

Education has long been viewed as the most important factor in counteracting the ignorance, denial, and stigma that fuel the STD epidemic. STD hotlines, the Internet websites, and government-issued

Phone operators with the Centers for Disease Control and Prevention take calls on their hot line. Educational agencies such as the CDC are very effective in combating the spread of STDs.

pamphlets at clinics and doctors' offices have all been helpful in providing up-to-date information about STDs and ways to prevent them. Yet these avenues for education are only partially effective as they mainly reach those who already have some awareness of or curiosity about STDs. Getting the message across to those with little or no knowledge of STDs poses a greater challenge but is critical for stemming the tide of new infections.

The high prevalence of STDs among teenagers has made this group one of the primary targets for educational campaigns about STDs. While there is a general consensus that alerting teens to the dangers of STDs is necessary, opinions are divided on how best to accomplish this. Parents and educators disagree about whom to teach, what information to present, and when educational programs should be offered. Traditionally the responsibility for discussing STDs, and sexuality in general, with children has been left to parents. The danger of this status quo is that not all parents are able, willing, or well enough informed to teach their children about STDs. Even when parents make the attempt to talk about STDs with their children, the effectiveness of discussions may be compromised by the parent-child relationship. Kathy, a high school student, says, "Both of my parents spoke to me about sex. I think they were mostly worried that I would become pregnant or get a disease, like AIDS. Even though I knew that what they were talking about was important and I wanted to know more, I felt uncomfortable about asking questions. I was worried that they might think that I was already having sex if I seemed too interested."[20] The fact is that while some teens may learn about STD prevention from their parents or doctors, most people in this age group say their school health programs are their primary source of information.

There is little question that school health-education programs are ideal for reaching the majority of teens, but accommodating the diverse personal and cultural values of all students is difficult at best. One of the central issues is whether school programs should provide students with information about all forms of STD prevention or only cover the option of sexual abstinence. Programs that teach abstinence, outside of marriage, as the only acceptable means of STD prevention have been heavily promoted by the

Teen girls listen attentively as their teacher explains the female reproductive system. Many schools are introducing instruction about STDs into the curriculum.

federal government over the past few years, with half a billion dollars allocated by Congress since 1998 and an expected increase to $133 million per year in 2003. In contrast, no federal funds are currently being put toward programs that teach comprehensive methods of STD prevention. As such, the number of schools teaching

schools to promote the message of sexual abstinence until marriage, many of these same parents want schools to include comprehensive methods of STD prevention in their programs. Tina Hoft, director of public health for the Kaiser foundation says, "What comes across in this study is that parents look to schools to prepare their children for real life. Their concerns are practical, not political."[22]

Education Is Essential

In the absence of cures for serious STDs, education is the main hope for arresting the STD epidemic. According to Debra Haffner, the president of the Sexuality Information and Education Council of the United States, "Abstinence and monogamy are 100% effective if they are practiced. But we know that [they] are not always practiced, even by people who say they are practicing them. . . . There are lots of studies that show that if you give people good education, they will protect themselves."[23]

Chapter 4

Living with AIDS

IN THE SPRING OF 1996 schoolteacher Beth Bye was extremely ill with the incurable sexually transmitted disease AIDS. Infected with the human immunodeficiency virus (HIV), which destroys the immune system, Beth's body was no longer able to fight off infections. She had suffered from a multitude of illnesses, most of which had been treated only to appear again, and she was now losing her vision and mental capacity. Beth was constantly tired and could no longer work or even take her dog for walks. On the advice of her doctor, Beth had already made arrangements for her own funeral and was considering entering a hospice in which to live out her few remaining days.

It was at this stage that Beth was given a newly developed therapy for AIDS. The effects were astounding. Within two months, the devastation that HIV had caused to her immune system had been significantly reversed. Beth was now able to take two-mile walks with her dog and even return to her thirty-hour-a-week teaching job. Beth says, "My recovery was like being on death row and getting that last minute pardon from the governor."[24] Though recovery from an extremely advanced stage of AIDS is not guaranteed, thanks to a better understanding of the disease and the advent of new treatments, AIDS patients are spending less time in hospitals and more time leading productive, rewarding, more normal lives.

A Complex Disease

New treatments for AIDS have taken a long time to develop, in part because AIDS is an extremely complex disease. Characterized by a failure of the body to fight off infection, AIDS typically

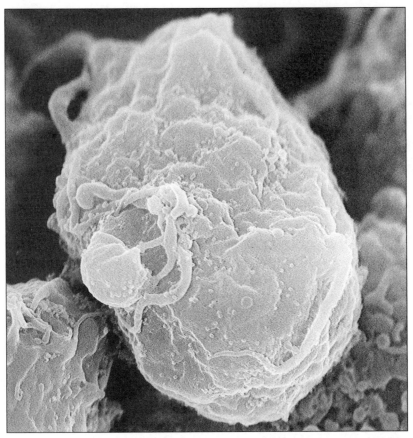

Shown here is an electron micrograph of the human immunodeficiency virus (HIV). HIV is spread through the exchange of bodily fluids or blood.

presents as a series of diseases, or syndrome, that is eventually fatal. HIV, the cause of AIDS, is spread through the exchange of bodily fluids or blood, occurring most frequently through sexual contact and the use of injectable drugs. Like other viruses, HIV requires a host cell to reproduce, but is unusual because it prefers cells of the human immune system, known as T-helper cells. Infection by HIV results in the death of these cells and the collapse of the immune system.

Destruction of the immune system takes time, and a diagnosis of AIDS might not be made for many years after infection by HIV. In the interim, symptoms vary widely from person to person with the only common sign being frequent and persistent illness. Eventually HIV reduces the number of T-helper cells below a critical level, disarming the immune system and leading to full-blown AIDS. At this point the body can no longer defend itself against the microbes that are a part of the natural environment and a continual string of opportunistic infections occur leading to death.

The randomness and repetition of opportunistic infections suffered by AIDS patients and the rapid deterioration in appearance, mental capacity, and basic motor skills are some of the aspects that AIDS patients and those around them find most difficult to cope with. Young, previously healthy people who would

A young patient in an advanced stage of AIDS suffers from an outbreak of lesions.

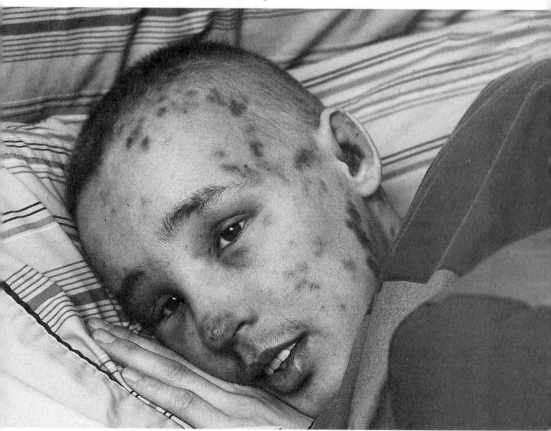

otherwise look forward to a long and active life may succumb to rare lung infections or cancers, suffer significant weight loss, or become permanently disabled from attacks to their nervous system.

Early detection of HIV is important because treatments that delay the downward spiral to AIDS are far more effective if they are started at an early stage of infection rather than at a point when the immune system is severely damaged. Diagnosis of HIV requires only a simple blood test that can be performed as early as six to twelve weeks after infection, yet many people are not diagnosed until much later. Some are unaware that they are infected with HIV and are only diagnosed when they fall ill. Others may suspect that they are infected, but find it difficult to confront this deadly disease by being tested. Tim, who was urged to be tested for HIV by his partner in 1985, remembers telling him, "I'm already fairly sure I am HIV positive. . . . I don't really need to carry around this burden of actually knowing. If I've got it, I've got it and I'm going to be dead in a couple of years anyway." [25]

Life-Altering HIV Diagnosis

Being diagnosed with HIV has a profound impact on most people's lives. It alters their self-image and the way others view them, resulting in a reassessment of personal goals and dramatic changes in relationships with friends and family. The imminent threat of death posed by a positive diagnosis is the impetus behind these changes. According to David, who is currently being treated for AIDS, "Fear of death is a difficult emotion for most of us to deal with but when the prospect is placed dramatically in front of you as with an AIDS diagnosis, it can lead to all sorts of desperate thinking." [26] Some become obsessed with finding a cure for their disease. Others react recklessly, taking illegal drugs, binge drinking, or frivolously spending their life's savings. Depression and loss of self-esteem are also common. Darlene, a forty-nine-year-old heterosexual grandmother, who discovered that she was HIV positive eight and a half years ago, had a typical response: "After [finding out about my] infection, I felt very much like damaged goods and worthless." [27]

A man holds a pair of signs condemning homosexuality. Many people mistakenly believe that only homosexuals and drug users spread AIDS.

The feelings of worthlessness experienced by people with HIV are often reinforced by the prejudices and biases of others. Although HIV can be spread by many different routes, those who are infected may be shunned by people who assume that their disease was contracted through homosexual activity or the use of illicit drugs, or who mistakenly fear contracting HIV from casual contact with the infected person. Though it is well known that HIV cannot be spread by casual contact, such as shaking hands or sharing food, many people are poorly informed or skeptical of this information. Steve, a social worker at an AIDS treatment center in New York, says, "People here still talk about going to visit families and having someone put a newspaper down on the couch for them to sit on, or wash their dishes with bleach after dinner."[28]

Positive results from an HIV test can sour a sexual relationship, regardless of whether the infection was acquired from that particular partner. Monica, who found out about her HIV infection in 1995, says, "The man I was seeing dropped me like a hot potato when he found out."[29] In contrast to worries about casual contact, the concerns of sexual partners are justified. Sexual intercourse is one of the most common ways that HIV is transmitted and even the use of condoms does not give 100 percent protection. Some people may continue to have sexual relations with an HIV-positive partner, but many others will consider the risk too great and will end the relationship.

Negative attitudes may also surface in the workplace despite the introduction of laws to prevent discrimination against people with HIV. One of the most difficult situations that Tim encountered was at work. Tim says, "The area manager went out of his way to make life as uncomfortable for me as he could, including taking me aside for a quiet coffee and telling me I should get out of the

---

HIV patients must seek medical treatment in the earliest stages of infection. Proper medical care is essential to ensure that the immune system continues to function.

job. If I'd only had a witness! But he was very clever and never said anything when anyone else was around."[30] Actions such as these are illegal in most places, but other laws permit discriminatory action against those with HIV. In April 1997 a law was passed granting the U.S. Immigration and Naturalization Services (INS) the right to arrest and remove any noncitizen who is HIV positive and who has entered the country without INS permission. Other countries have similar policies and require proof of HIV-negative status before granting residency or citizenship.

Taking Control of HIV

Living with HIV requires infected people to both manage the upheaval brought on by diagnosis and seek treatment for their disease, with one goal: keeping the immune system functioning as well as possible for as long as possible. Management of HIV is complex because both physical and emotional health must be taken into account. Staying physically healthy requires constant medical attention, while stable emotional health hinges on keeping stress and disruptive change to a minimum. Finding a balance between the two can be tricky. David, who is HIV positive, says:

> I have taken the view that I will try to live my life in as normal a way as possible compared to life before HIV. To try and develop a moderate middle-of-the-road approach to a potentially alarming dilemma without getting too carried away. Sometimes with a multitude of opportunistic infections it has been difficult to do. After each new infection I have tried to incorporate the new extra pills with a minimum of fuss and depression. . . . Self-pity and the melodrama of AIDS are the enemies to be avoided where possible. Of course it doesn't always work. Attend a couple of funerals in a month and you realize you're in a pretty bizarre, almost surreal situation. The bone seems pointed squarely in your direction as the coffin is carried down the aisle.[31]

Good medical care is essential for survival and ideally should begin in the earliest, asymptomatic period of HIV infection. Early care is focused on eliminating the threat of opportunistic infections before the immune system is destroyed. Vaccination against diseases such as hepatitis B and detection and treatment of undiagnosed diseases prevents them from becoming deadly threats later on. A close watch is also kept on the condition of the immune system. Frequent testing is performed to determine the number of T-helper cells per milliliter of blood. This provides a measure of how far the disease has progressed and helps forecast when treatment should begin in order to prevent opportunistic infections from getting the upper hand. Because treatment of HIV is complex and requires constant and long-term medical attention, many AIDS patients find selecting a doctor and medical team with suitable expertise and with whom they are comfortable makes a big difference in their ability to follow treatment regimens.

Yet finding a good doctor does not necessarily mean that the infected person can sit back and relax. Recent studies show that people who live the longest are those who take an active interest in learning how to treat HIV from a variety of sources rather than leaving all of the decisions up to their doctor.

Miraculous New Drugs for HIV Are Only a Partial Solution

Drug treatments for HIV have dramatically improved with the introduction in 1996 of a combination drug therapy called highly active antiretroviral therapy (HAART). Prior to this time most people with HIV died within a few years of contracting the virus. However, since the advent of HAART it is now common for infected people to live relatively active lives for ten years or more. Because of this new therapy, AIDS-related deaths in the United States plummeted from fifty thousand in 1995 to well under twenty thousand in the year 2000. HAART works by decreasing the number of viral particles inside the body, thereby restoring immune function. According to Richard Klein, of the Food and Drug Administration, "It returns many who were dead and dying to a relatively healthy and productive life."[32] The impact that HAART can have on a person's health is so dramatic that it is often referred to as the "Lazarus effect" in reference to the biblical figure who was raised from the dead.

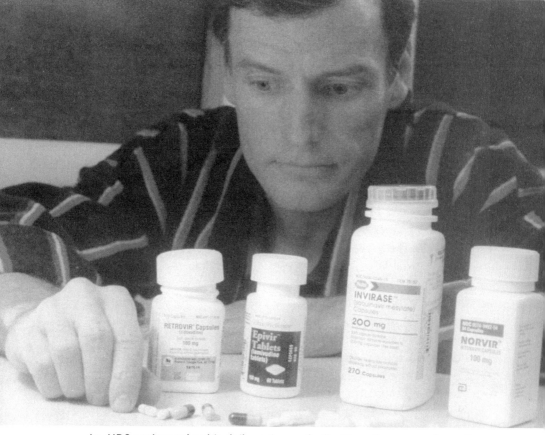

An AIDS patient takes his daily regimen of pills. Drug therapy prolongs the lives of many AIDS patients.

The new drugs for HIV may be successful at improving the health and increasing the longevity of those infected with HIV, but they are not for everyone and they involve significant difficulties. One problem is that they are expensive. Treatment of a single person with HAART costs between seven and twenty thousand dollars per year. While insurance companies may pay part or all of the bill for their clients, people who do not have insurance can find access to treatment difficult.

Demanding dosing schedules and side effects are also problematic. A minimum of three types of medication are involved in HAART therapy. These must be taken several times a day and at specific times in relation to meals and other medications. Forgetting to take the medications or taking them at the wrong times can have disastrous consequences, allowing viral numbers to rebound and encouraging the evolution of drug-resistant strains. Because of these dangers, some doctors encourage their patients do a practice run using jelly beans or mints to see if they can stick to the schedule. Even when medications are taken correctly, serious side effects are common and may even force discontinuing the treatment. The least serious side effects include chronic diarrhea and an unsightly redistribution of fat from the face and limbs to the stomach, breasts, and neck. HAART can also induce diabetes, strokes, and heart attacks, as well as increase the likelihood of bleeding in hemophiliacs.

However, the most disappointing aspect of HAART is that it is ultimately unable to cure HIV. While HAART is successful in reducing HIV to undetectable levels in the blood of patients, it is only a temporary reprieve from the disease because the virus remains untouched in areas such as the brain, retina, and testes and inevitably becomes resistant to the drugs. At this point, therapy becomes ineffective, viral numbers increase, and the progression to AIDS is resumed.

The difficulties brought on by the treatment of HIV make many question whether the advantages in prolonging life are worth the trouble. When Tim first began HAART in 1997, he was taking 357 tablets a week. Some of these were to control the side effects from the drugs themselves, including chronic diarrhea. Doctors would enthusiastically announce Tim's rising T-helper cell counts and decreasing viral loads, but Tim found the regimen almost too difficult to bear, commenting:

> I'm getting all of these benefits from it but. . . . are the benefits really worth the quality of life that I'm being deprived of? Three hundred odd drugs for 12 months or for 2 years or for 10 years? Of course if you're going to take that many drugs over a long period of time, you really need a hell of a lot of motivation and good health isn't a good enough motivation on its own to take a huge amount of drugs, particularly when you're getting side effects from them.[33]

Indeed, toxic side effects and inability to tolerate the HAART regimen lead many patients to discontinue it or switch to a different "drug cocktail" in as little as four months. Some people would rather face the consequences of HIV than those of HAART and most long for a less grueling treatment option.

Alternative Therapies and Healthy Living

In an effort to lessen the side effects, increase toleration of HAART, and improve their general sense of strength and well-being, many people living with HIV have turned to alternative therapies. Massage, acupuncture, herbal remedies, and homeopathy are some of the treatments that have been documented as offering relief from medication side effects and AIDS-related symptoms. In addition, there is evidence that people who receive these types of therapy feel healthier for taking an active role in their own medical treatment.

Healthy living can also strengthen the immune system. A balanced diet that includes the four food groups—protein, fruits and vegetables, breads and cereals, and dairy products—is important for people infected with HIV because it provides the body with energy to fight the virus. Most people with HIV need a minimum of thirty-five hundred calories per day and a protein intake that is one and a half to two times greater than is recommended for uninfected people. Some foods that are not recommended for the uninfected are actually good for people with HIV: Ice cream, pizza, tacos, and hamburgers, besides stimulating the appetite, can be valuable sources of protein and their high calorie and fat content helps counteract the weight loss associated with HIV infection.

The diet of people with HIV may need to be modified when certain illnesses arise. More calories may be required to combat a fever, and high fat or sugary foods may need to be temporarily abandoned to fight off some opportunistic infections. Diarrhea can undermine good nutrition by flushing valuable nutrients out of the body before they are absorbed. Special supplements with high fat, protein, and carbohydrate content may need to be taken if the condition continues.

Factors that stress the body also need to be eliminated so that the immune system is not further taxed and can devote all of its energies to fighting HIV. Getting a good night's sleep can be very helpful, as can moderate exercise. Smoking cigarettes and using recreational drugs is particularly damaging to HIV-positive individuals and is strongly discouraged.

Staying Emotionally Connected

When it comes to weathering the effects of HIV, taking care of emotional health is every bit as important as physical health. Coping with the psychological effects from HIV infection is no small feat. The initial shock of diagnosis is often followed by difficult treatment, unpredictable infections, and traumatic changes to a person's social life. Without support, the situation can easily become overwhelming and undermine any physical improvements gained from drug therapy. "I see [emotional] support as a vital HIV long-

Emotional support from family and friends is vital to the survival of people infected with AIDS.

term survival skill," says Darlene, who is infected with HIV. "Without all of the support I have received, I sincerely believe I would not be here today."[34]

Indeed, research shows a strong correlation between the longevity of people infected with HIV and their ability to establish a network of emotional support. It does not matter whether the network members are composed of partners, friends, family, or HIV support groups, as long as they are sympathetic and can maintain an emotional connection with the infected person. However, forming a support network is not always easy for people with HIV because it requires them to tell others about their infection. Sonja, who is infected with HIV, says, "Telling my family, in particular my parents, was one of the hardest things I have ever had to do. Not only did I have to tell them that I was HIV positive but also that I was an injecting drug user. Something that I had kept hidden for many years."[35]

At a time when they are already emotionally fragile, people with HIV need to be selective about whom they tell. Sonja found it liberating to publish an article about her infection in a newspaper, but she cautions people to think carefully before disclosing their HIV-positive status. Sonja says:

> Being clear within yourself about what sort of support you need and whom can best provide it will help you with disclosing. Ask yourself who needs to know and why they need to know. . . . Telling others can be life altering and sometimes painful so think carefully before you go exposing your soul to the world and be sure to have some sort of net in place to catch you if you should happen to topple unexpectedly. If you have a negative response from someone whom you thought would have responded differently don't let it dissuade you from seeking support from friends, support workers or counsellors.[36]

Many people with HIV form their closest friendships with people who are also HIV positive. It is easier to relate to and empathize with people who have undergone the same major life experience. Meeting people who are HIV positive is not difficult. Numerous sites on the Internet promote communication between HIV-positive people. In addition, most medical institutions that offer treatment for HIV also organize HIV-positive support groups. Not only do these groups provide emotional support, but they help their members keep abreast of the latest treatments and may arrange assisted-living services when people become too ill to live independently.

Leading a Normal Life

As long as their health remains sound, there is no reason why people with HIV cannot exercise, work, attend school, and socialize just like everyone else. Striving to return to a normal life in spite of all of the demands of the disease may be one of the healthiest moves that a person with HIV makes. Readjusting to normal life does not necessarily happen overnight. It may take time to come to terms with the disease and have the energy and desire to pursue normal activities. Darlene remembers reaching the turning point:

> When I was first diagnosed, I found nothing funny at all about HIV/AIDS. . . . I got aggravated when someone would try to joke about it. How dare they laugh at this terrible disease or about anything was my thoughts. However, that began to change when I attended my first AIDS retreat six months after I was diagnosed. I actually started seeing PWA's [people with AIDS] laughing and having fun in spite of being positive. I didn't understand how anyone could possibly be having fun and enjoying life when they had a disease that would some day kill them; but, I knew that I wanted to be able to laugh and enjoy life again just like they were. I heard that "laugher is like medicine to the soul" most of my life but at this retreat this phrase took on a new meaning. I needed to be able to take life with a grain of salt and enjoy it in spite of living with HIV.[37]

Decisions about returning to work or school are basic to resuming life as a person with HIV. Keeping a job, for example, might be not only financially necessary but extremely gratifying as well: Work provides a distraction from the disease and the chance to interact with other people. There is no field of work that people with HIV are restricted from entering. Eight years after being diagnosed with

HIV, Chris decided to return to her former profession as a caterer. Although it is illegal for employers to discriminate against HIV-positive job applicants or employees, Chris was nervous about how people would feel about her handling food if they found out about her infection. Her first day back at work was difficult, she says: "The butterflies were doing back flips when I first walked in, but subsided by the end of my shift. The work is only part-time, but it has boosted my self-esteem ten-fold. . . . I feel absolutely exhausted after I have finished work, but it is nice to be able to confidently say that it is because of work and not the effects of HIV."[38]

Assisted living provides HIV and AIDS patients with a safe, caring environment in which they can receive the most current treatments available.

Sexual relationships are part of normal life for most adults, whether they are infected with HIV or not. However, the dangers of transmission during sex means that the safety of sexual partners must be given serious consideration. Using condoms correctly and consistently is not good enough. Being responsible means making sure that potential partners are aware of the infection before becoming sexually involved. Although hearing this news will discourage many people from continuing the relationship, it is important that they are informed of the risk so that they can help with the careful use of condoms if they choose to pro-

Using condoms correctly and regularly is essential to stopping the spread of STDs.

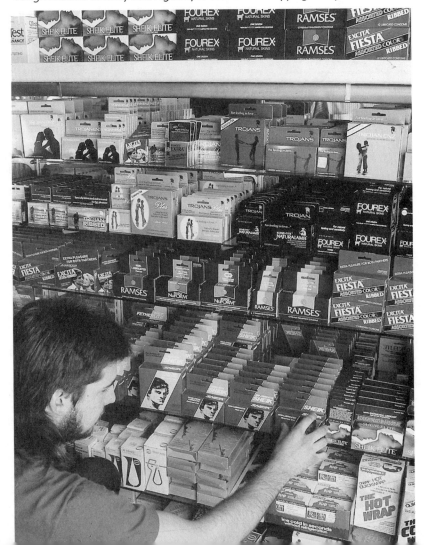

ceed. One way to stop HIV from being an obstacle to intimate relationships is to choose partners who are also HIV positive, and support networks such as dating services that deal exclusively with HIV-positive clients are in place as sources of introduction and social interaction.

For some people living with HIV/AIDS, sexual activity and sexual desire wanes as a side effect of medication and illness, especially as the disease progresses. While drugs such as Viagra and injections of testosterone can be successful in boosting the sex drive, some HIV-positive people find emotional closeness may take precedence over physical satisfaction and prefer to adopt a celibate lifestyle.

"A Double-Edged Sword"

Living with HIV may seem like a relentless struggle to stay alive and healthy, but in the midst of coping with the difficult consequences of HIV, many people find a new appreciation for life. One person infected with HIV expresses this philosophy as measuring life by its depth, not its length. Being forced to confront mortality day in and day out can get people to focus on the things that are really important and make positive changes sooner rather than later. Tim is one person who sees a positive side to his infection. Reflecting on his current situation, Tim says:

> I don't know how much longer I'm going to live. I could live another 30 years. I view HIV as a double-edged sword. I hate having HIV because it made me very ill [and] I've lost so many friends that I don't even talk about it because it's so heartbreaking. So I hate it for those reasons. But I love it because if it hadn't happened, I'd still be doing this job that I hate and I would just be living my life on that level. I wouldn't have gone through that huge transformation. That huge 'I don't want to do that anymore, I want to go off and do this.' And I would not have taken on board things that I want to do instead of what people thought I had to do or what my parents thought I should do. So 20 years on, its like I've been given a new life. It's very wonderful. [39]

Chapter 5

The Future of STDs

S TARTING WITH THE discovery of antibiotics by Alexander Fleming in 1929, the last century has uncovered an unprecedented number of cures for human diseases, including STDs. As a result, the fatality rates for STDs such as syphilis and gonorrhea have plummeted. Significant advances have also been made in the diagnosis and treatment of many STDs. Yet, in spite these successes, the number of people infected with STDs has never been higher, and the emergence of AIDS has made STDs one of the fastest-growing and most well-funded focuses of medical research.

There are good reasons for seeking new and more effective treatments for STDs. One is the appearance of new strains of drug-resistant organisms against which previously successful treatments have less and less effect. Because bacteria are extremely adept at transferring their drug-resistant abilities to their drug-sensitive neighbors, antibiotic resistance is occurring more and more frequently among the bacteria that cause gonorrhea, syphilis, chlamydia, and chancroid. Overuse of these drugs has contributed to this problem. For example, penicillin used to be commonly taken by prostitutes to ward off possible infection by gonorrhea. Taking this antibiotic as a precaution, rather than a cure, encouraged the growth of drug resistant organisms. As a result, most strains of gonorrhea are now resistant to penicillin, and it is not uncommon to find strains with resistance to two or three antibiotics.

Although there are still a number of antibiotics that can be effectively used against gonorrhea and other bacterial STDs, over the last decade bacteria that are resistant to every known antibiotic have been isolated from sick patients. Infections of this type are difficult to treat and often impossible to cure and are on the rise. According to Hazel Mitchell, an expert in the epidemiology of human disease at the University of New South Wales in Sydney, Australia, "There is a great need for new antibiotics which act in a novel manner. If new treatments are not found soon, we may see a regression back to the days where a cut on a finger could result in a fatal infection."[40]

New Drugs Are Rare

Finding new drugs to use against STDs is difficult, sometimes extraordinarily so. For every one that works, tens of thousands of synthetic and naturally occurring chemical compounds may have been considered. Clement Stone, a former senior vice president of research for Merck, a pharmaceuticals giant, says, "Each drug has its own way of being born. Often we consciously search for a drug

Improper use of antibiotics over time has created strains of diseases that are resistant to drugs, like this strain of gonorrhea.

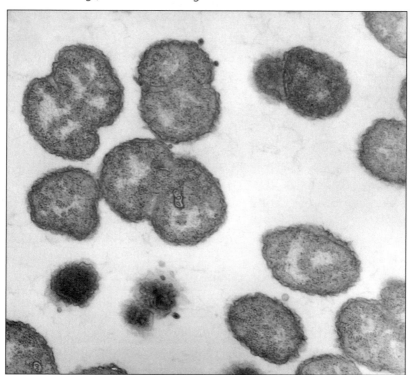

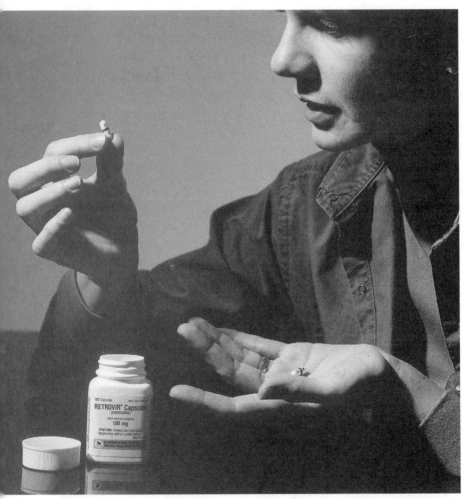

AZT was originally developed as a cancer treatment, but it proved to be ineffective. Fortunately, it is helpful in retarding the progression of AIDS.

for a specific use, but more often it is serendipity."[41] The use of AZT, the first antiviral drug to have a substantial effect on HIV, is a case in point. This drug was originally examined as a treatment for cancer in 1964 but did not turn out to be useful. It was not until the 1980s, some twenty years later, that AZT was found to slow the progression of HIV infection to AIDS.

Even after a drug is found to be effective in the laboratory, it must go through a rigorous and lengthy testing process to prove that it is safe in humans. According to the Pharmaceutical Research and Manufacturers of America organization, out of five thousand compounds that enter preclinical testing, only five will make it to human trials and approximately one out of those five will be found to be effective and safe enough to be approved for public use. On average, it takes 8.5 years of testing to get a drug to market. This is a very long time when compared to the rate at which germs are becoming drug resistant.

Relatively accelerated approval of AIDS drugs is the one exception to the lengthy process of drug approval. Realizing that many people facing a certain death are willing to gamble on the success of an unproven and possibly dangerous treatment, the Food and Drug Administration issued new guidelines that loosen the strict controls on safety in humans that are part of the drug-testing process. Fully informed of possible health risks, HIV-positive individuals can participate in clinical trials of experimental drugs that otherwise might not have reached the human trial stage for years. The

This AIDS patient has participated in many clinical drug trials since he first contracted the disease in the early 1980s.

benefits are two-fold; people with HIV gain early access to the latest treatments, while the assessment of new drugs is accelerated by a large supply of volunteers.

Immunotherapy: An Untapped Resource

Not all of the new treatments rely on the discovery of conventional drugs. Some of the most exciting new prospects for treating STDs are based on the knowledge of ways that the body itself can be prompted to fight an existing infection. A new line of treatment, called immunotherapy or therapeutic vaccination, is being devised to make use of this untapped resource. It works by the topical application or injection of substances that trigger a change in the immune system, causing it to eliminate the infection from the body or render the germs inactive.

While immunotherapy commonly makes use of drugs, it differs from conventional treatments because the body does most of the work and the drugs only need to be administered once or infrequently. This makes it ideal for improving the treatment of STDs that currently require long-term, daily doses of medication. According to a senior scientist in charge of therapeutic vaccine development for a large pharmaceutical company:

> Market research shows that many people with STDs do not like to take pills to control their condition. It reminds them day in and day out that they are infected with an STD. There is also the worry that their pills will be discovered by other people. Cutting down on the demands of a treatment by swapping a daily dose of pills for infrequent injections or a cream that is rubbed into the skin makes it more appealing and solves the problem of people forgetting to take their medicine or taking the wrong amount. [42]

This change in how some STD drugs are administered could have a major impact on the current epidemic by increasing compliance as well as relieving infected people of their symptoms and making them less contagious to others.

Immunotherapy research for several STDs is well under way. Two such treatments for genital herpes are in the later stages of development and are showing great promise. In recent clinical trials, both treatments, one that is given by injection and the other that works as a topical gel, were found to stop or reduce the frequency of recurrent herpes outbreaks for up to six months following treatment. This is a substantial advance over the daily oral doses of antiviral drugs taken by many people to keep their symptoms under control. Positive data has also been reported for an immunotherapy agent for genital warts in males, clearing warts and reducing the chances of relapse in a high percentage of men who participated in a trial.

Hope that a therapeutic vaccine is possible for HIV stems from the fact that a small percentage of people infected with HIV are so-called long-term nonprogressors, meaning that they have lived with the infection for two decades or more without getting sick and without treatment. Some especially powerful immune response in these people is preventing the virus from causing harm, and researchers are trying to identify the chemical or genetic factors that contribute to that response in hopes of duplicating it in the laboratory.

Several therapeutic vaccines for HIV are being tested in clinical trials with human subjects. The most promising results have come in subjects whose viral loads have already been reduced with antiviral drugs, but a therapeutic vaccine has already been shown to benefit monkeys infected with SIV, a virus that is closely related to HIV, and results from ongoing trials in humans are expected in 2003. Another therapeutic vaccine developed against chlamydia has not yet been tested in humans, but it has been found to work in mice, and researchers are hopeful that it will also work in primates.

An Ounce of Prevention Is Worth a Pound of Cure

New treatments for STDs may be on the way, but past experience shows that they may not be sufficient to halt the current epidemic. The problem is that STDs spread from person to person so rapidly that even when a cure exists, it cannot be administered quickly enough to counteract the number of new infections.

Relying on cures alone is problematic from an economic standpoint as well. The development and licensing of new drugs is so costly that few new drugs can be priced affordably in the poor countries of the developing world, where the incidence of STDs is highest and the treatments are most sorely needed. Aside from the moral issues that this raises, cures that are only available to a fortunate few will not be of great benefit in reducing the incidence of STDs because they do little to stop the diseases from circulating throughout the population. A separate economic issue is the vast amount of money that could be saved on health care if STDs were avoided in the first place. For all these reasons, finding new ways to prevent STDs is every bit as important as finding cures.

On the forefront of STD prevention is the move to produce topical creams or gels that can kill the germs that cause STDs. Over sixty of these products, also called microbicides, are currently under development. Most of these are being designed to work by the preintercourse application of the product within the vagina, preventing the transmission of STDs. The fact that these microbicides can be used without the knowledge or consent of a male partner is seen as a bonus since females in many cultures are prevented from using protective devices, such as condoms, by their male partners. Yet in some ways, microbicides are not a great improvement over existing forms of prevention. Like condoms, they can only be effective if they are used for every act of intercourse. Forgetting to use them or using them incorrectly even once is enough to contract an STD.

Vaccines to Protect Against STDs

Vaccines are some of the best forms of disease prevention because they deliver effective, long-lasting protection with only one or a limited series of injections and can be administered to healthy populations before any infection occurs. Most of the major health organizations see the development of vaccines as essential for bringing the STD epidemic and other diseases under control. According to Anthony S. Fauci, the director of the National Institute

AIDS activists in Spain rally to demand affordable medical treatment for developing countries.

of Allergy and Infectious Diseases, "Our commitment to developing new and better vaccines to prevent the world's most serious infectious diseases has never been stronger."[43]

Although the concept for vaccines is not new, hepatitis B is the only STD for which a vaccine is currently available. While it would be ideal to develop a vaccine for every STD, limited resources mean that priority is given to the STDs that pose the greatest threat. Vaccines to protect against cervical cancer, genital warts, genital herpes, and HIV have received the most attention since there are no cures for these diseases. A vaccine for genital herpes is within reach, with the final stage of clinical trials under way in the United States. One study shows that the vaccine gives good protection, preventing genital herpes infection in 73 percent of uninfected women over the nineteen-month duration of the study. However, the vaccine has several limitations. One is that the vaccine does not work well in women who are already infected with a related strain of herpes that causes cold sores. Another is that, for reasons researchers do not understand, it also does not work

A researcher works to develop an AIDS vaccine. Despite the fact that considerable medical research has been devoted to AIDS, no effective vaccine exists.

in men. Despite these shortcomings, researchers feel that use of this vaccine will provide powerful ammunition against the herpes epidemic. Lawrence R. Stanberry, one of the developers of the vaccine, says, "If you did universal vaccination of 11- and 12-year-old women you would eventually see an impact on the spread of herpes in both men and women."[44] According to Stanberry, the vaccine will also be beneficial for decreasing the number of babies infected by the genital herpes virus at birth.

A significant breakthrough is being hailed in the development of vaccines against HPV, the virus responsible for cervical cancer and genital warts. In recent clinical trials, a vaccine that targets the strain of HPV that causes most cases of cervical cancer protected 100 percent of the nearly twenty-four hundred women that received it. In an editorial that accompanied the published results of the trials, physician Christopher Crum wrote that the new HPV vaccine heralds "the beginning of the end for cervical cancer."[45] An even more potent version of the vaccine, aimed at two cervical-cancer-causing strains and two strains that cause genital warts, is currently in clinical trials in thirteen different countries. The vaccine, which may be widely available in as little as five years, will be given to females before they become sexually active.

Advances in HIV Vaccine Development

The devastating effects of HIV and the lack of affordable drug treatment has resulted in the development of a phenomenal number of experimental HIV vaccines reaching the stage of human trials. Since 1987 there have been over fifty-two clinical trials involving over twenty-seven different vaccines. Thus far, however, not one has been found to be effective for preventing infection by HIV.

The reason for this difficulty is that HIV has a high mutation rate that gives rise to numerous new strains of HIV, each with unique surface structures. Because preventative vaccines work by preparing the body to identify and attack germs based on their specific surface structures, it is a major challenge to produce a single vaccine that will reliably prevent infection by all strains of HIV.

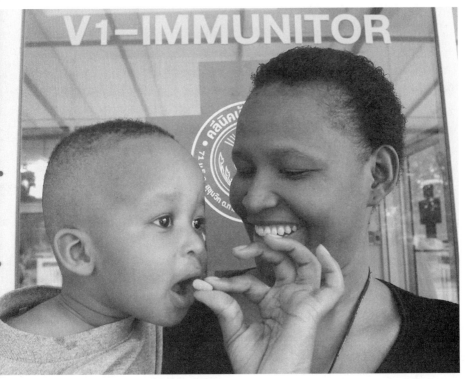

An HIV-positive mother in Thailand gives her son an experimental AIDS vaccine in the form of a pill. Many people are hopeful about such experimental drugs.

However, trying to turn this feature to their advantage, some researchers are working to devise a vaccine that can outwit the virus by causing it to mutate so rapidly that it can no longer survive. Such a vaccine has been shown to protect laboratory monkeys from subsequent exposure to SIV, and human trials are presently being conducted in the United States, Thailand, Trinidad, Haiti, Brazil, and Uganda.

Genome Sequencing Technology Assists in the Fight Against STDs

Perhaps the greatest contribution to the fight against STDs has been the development of revolutionary genetic technology that makes it possible to map the entire DNA sequence, or genome, of an organism. The genomes of organisms that cause STDs were among the first to be sequenced. Genomes from the germs that cause chancroid, gonorrhea, syphilis, and chlamydia, as well as herpes, genital warts, hepatitis B, and HIV have been completed. Encoding all of the instructions for the growth and function of an organism, the genome sequence is viewed as an invaluable tool in the design of new cures, treatments, and methods of prevention.

The benefits of gene sequencing for drug development can already be seen for HIV. Completion of this genome in the mid-1990s allowed two critical steps in the viral life cycle to be identified. Drugs were then found that blocked these steps, interfering with

A lab worker conducts AIDS research. Gene sequencing is leading researchers in promising new directions that may yield solutions to the epidemic of sexually transmitted diseases.

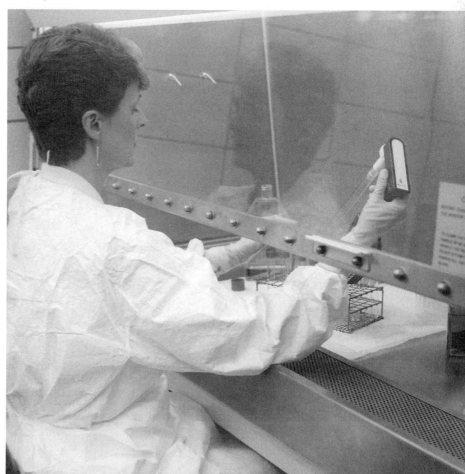

viral replication. The end result was the development of the effective treatment known as HAART, which has greatly improved the health and longevity of people infected with HIV.

Gene sequencing also speeds the process of trying to develop effective vaccines against STDs. Because a vaccine is derived from proteins that exist on the surface, or exterior, of the infectious organism's "body," knowing which proteins exist on the surface and which exist in its interior tells researchers specifically which proteins to target for vaccine development. Genome data gives researchers that knowledge. Although no vaccine has yet been developed to prevent syphilis, the generation of the complete genome of *Treponema pallidum,* the organism that causes syphilis, has been hailed as a promising step in this direction. NIAID director Anthony S. Fauci says, "Completion of this project is an extraordinary boost for efforts to develop a protective vaccine."[46]

In April 2003 the Human Genome Project announced the completion of the mapping of the entire human genome. This much-heralded achievement means STD researchers can focus as never before on the mechanism of infection in the human host as well as the way the STD germs work. It may be possible to determine, for example, that some humans are genetically more susceptible to STD infection than others, and someday to medically remedy that vulnerability. Understanding STDs from the perspective of both disease germs and the humans that they infect will shed light on the best ways to fight them and the most effective ways to bring the STD epidemic under control.

Notes

Chapter 1: STDs: A Common Cause for Concern
1. Quoted in Linda Carroll, "Adam: A Man's Guide to Sexual Health," MSNBC News, September 3, 2000. www.msnbc.com.
2. Quoted in Centers for Disease Control and Prevention, "CDC Issues New Report on STD Epidemics," press release, December 5, 2000. www.cdc.gov.
3. Connie, interview by author, December 3, 2000, San Francisco, CA.
4. Connie, interview.
5. Quoted in Carroll, "Adam."

Chapter 2: Diagnosis and Treatment of STDs
6. Tom, interview by author, December 3, 2000, San Francisco, CA.
7. Quoted in Cheryl Wetzstein, "Certain STDs Reach Highs," *Insight on the News*, November 16, 1998. www.findarticles.com.
8. Quoted in "A Painful Lesson: Anyone Can Get Herpes," Sex, Etc., Winter 1998. www.sxetc.com.
9. Quoted in Anupama Mehta, "Messing with Myths About Genital Warts," Sex, Etc., Fall 1998. www.sxetc.com.
10. Quoted in Mehta, "Messing with Myths About Genital Warts."

Chapter 3: The Challenge of Prevention
11. Quoted in Sam Perdue, "NIAID Releases *The Jordan Report: Accelerated Development of Vaccines*," NIAID news release, August 31, 2001. www.niaid.nih.gov.
12. Connie, interview.
13. David Satcher, *The Surgeon General's Call to Action to Promote Sexual Health and Responsible Sexual Behavior*, Office of the Surgeon General, June 28, 2001. www.surgeongeneral.gov.

14. Quoted in Jonathan Cedeno, "Feel Like You're the Last American Virgin? (You're Not)," Sex, Etc., December 17, 2001. www.sxetc.com.
15. Thom Pasculli, "To Be or Not To Be a Virgin? Sex Is . . . Sacred," Sex, Etc., December 17, 2001. www.sxetc.com.
16. Quoted in *Milwaukee Journal Sentinel*, "Many Teens Underestimate STDs," ABC News, March 8, 1999. http://more.abcnews.go.com.
17. Quoted in *Milwaukee Journal Sentinel*, "Many Teens Underestimate STDs."
18. Tim Alderman, interview by author, December 20, 2001, Sydney, Australia.
19. Connie, interview by author.
20. Kathy, interview by author, October 8, 2002, Sydney, Australia.
21. Leslie M. Kantor and William F. Bacon, "Abstinence-Only Programs Implemented Under Welfare Reform Are Incompatible with Research on Effective Sexuality Education," *JAMWA*, vol. 57, no. 1, Winter 2002.
22. Quoted in Kaiser Family Foundation, "National Study on Sex Education Reveals Gaps Between What Parents Want and Schools Think," news release, September 26, 2000. www.kff.org.
23. Quoted in Wetzstein, "Certain STDs Reach Highs."

Chapter 4: Living with AIDS
24. Quoted in John Henkel, "Attacking AIDS with a 'Cocktail' Therapy," *FDA Consumer Magazine*, July–August 1999. www.fda.gov.
25. Alderman, video interview.
26. David Menadue, "Is Your Future in the Stars?" *Positive Living*, August 2002, Positive Stories, website. www.hivaids.webcentral.com.au.
27. Darlene Bouse, "Damaged Goods," HIV—First person, AEGIS, November 3, 2002. www.aegis.com.
28. Quoted in Paula Span, "Living with AIDS," *Washington Post Magazine*, May 27, 2001. www.washingtonpost.com.
29. Monica, personal story, Avert.org, HIV, December 1, 2002. www.avert.org.
30. Alderman, video interview.
31. Menadue, "Is Your Future in the Stars?"

32. Quoted in Henkel, "Attacking AIDS with a 'Cocktail' Therapy."
33. Alderman, video interview.
34. Bouse, "Damaged Goods."
35. Sonja, "Disclosure: When and How," Positive Women Victoria, HIV/AIDS Positive Stories, November 3, 2002. www.hivaids.webcentral.com.au.
36. Sonja, "Disclosure."
37. Bouse, "Damaged Goods."
38. Chris, "To Work or Not to Work," HIV/AIDS Positive Stories, November 3, 2002. www.hivaids.webcentral.com.au.
39. Alderman, video interview.

Chapter 5: The Future of STDs

40. Hazel Mitchell, interview by author, December 4, 2001, Sydney, Australia.
41. Quoted in Jeffrey P. Cohn, "The Beginnings: Laboratory and Animal Studies," *FDA Consumer Special Report*, January 1995. www.fda.gov.
42. Phil, interview by author, December 10, 2002, Melbourne, Australia.
43. Quoted in Perdue, "NIAID Releases *The Jordan Report*."
44. Quoted in BBC News, "Genital Herpes Vaccine Breakthrough," November 22, 2002. http://news.bbc.co.uk.
45. Quoted in Paul D. Blumenthal, "Immunization Against Cervical Cancer: Who? When? Where?" *Medscape Women's Health Journal*, November 11, 2002. www.medscape.com.
46. Quoted in June Wyman, "Syphilis Genome Sequence Offers Clues To Better Diagnosis, Prevention and Treatment," NIH, news release, July 16, 1998. www.nih.gov.

Glossary

abstinence: Voluntarily refraining from or avoiding sexual activity, also called celibacy.

antibiotics: Chemical substances that kill bacteria or inhibit bacterial growth.

antibodies: Proteins of the immune system that recognize foreign material and germs and help to destroy or eliminate them from the body.

asymptomatic: A disease state characterized by an absence of noticeable symptoms.

bacterium: A microscopic, single-celled, living organism. Bacteria can be found nearly everywhere including on the skin and within the gastrointestinal tract of humans. Most do not cause disease, but several are the infectious agents of STDs.

blood transfusion: A medically supervised procedure of replacing blood by injecting it into the veins.

cancer: The uncontrolled growth of cells within an animal.

CDC: Centers for Disease Control and Prevention; a U.S. federal agency located in Atlanta, Georgia, committed to the statistical tracking, control, and prevention of infectious disease.

celibacy: Abstaining from sexual intercourse.

chancre: An open sore; one of the symptoms of syphilis, the STD caused by *T. pallidum.*

cirrhosis: Liver disease, usually chronic and progressive, with fibrosis and nodule formation leading to liver failure.

condom: A thin, tight-fitting sheath worn over the penis or within the vagina to prevent pregnancy or STD transmission.

cryotherapy: A medical procedure that involves freezing, often by using liquid nitrogen.

culture: The provision of nutrients and appropriate conditions used to grow cells, tissue, or microscopic organisms in a laboratory.

DNA sequence: The "blueprint" for the synthesis of proteins and the function, growth, and replication of the cell, contained in the DNA (deoxyribonucleic acid) of the cell's nucleus.

drug resistance: The genetically acquired ability of microbes to resist the therapeutic effects of drugs such as antibiotics.

epidemic: A disease occurring in an unusually large number of people at the same time.

FDA: Food and Drug Administration; U.S. regulatory agency that oversees the testing, approval, and licensing of drugs for human use.

genome: The entire DNA sequence of a living organism.

germ: Microscopic living organism that causes disease.

HAART: Highly active antiretroviral therapy. A variable combination of usually three drugs whose coordinated effects inhibit HIV infection.

HIV: Human immunodeficiency virus, the cause of the sexually transmitted disease AIDS.

HPV: Human papillomavirus, the cause of the STD genital warts.

HSV: Herpes simplex virus, the cause of the STD genital herpes.

immune system: All of the components related to the body's defenses against foreign agents and disease, including the lymph nodes, lymphatic circulatory system, and the blood cells and antibodies that circulate throughout the body.

immunotherapy: A therapy, also known as a therapeutic vaccine, that alters the immune response in order to improve its ability to fight a disease.

infertility: The inability of males or females to conceive or bear children.

intracellular: Inside of a cell.

intravenous: Inside of a vein.

microbe: An organism that is microscopic in size, including viruses, bacteria, protozoa, and some fungi.

molecular: Processes or structures at the level of molecules, the basic chemical building blocks of all living and nonliving matter.

mucosal tissue: Mucus-secreting tissue within the eyes, inside the nose and mouth, and lining the reproductive and gastrointestinal tracts; the moist, soft nature of mucosal tissue makes it ideal ground for the transmission and growth of STDs.

NIAID: National Institute of Allergy and Infectious Diseases; supports scientific research aimed at developing better ways to diagnose, treat, and prevent infectious, immunologic, and allergic diseases.

NIH: National Institutes of Health; the world's largest medical research center, located in Bethesda, Maryland. Its primary function is to address health concerns in the United States by directing and promoting research into key areas.

opportunistic infection: Infections arising from microorganisms that are normally present on or near the body but are efficiently eliminated by a healthy immune system before they can cause disease. An impaired immune system thus provides "opportunity" for otherwise ineffective organisms to cause disease.

organism: A single-celled or multicellular life form.

PID: Pelvic inflammatory disease; a common complication of STDs in females.

protozoan: A microscopic one-celled organism that is the infectious agent for the STD trichomoniasis.

replicate: To make multiple copies.

STD: Sexually transmitted disease; an infectious disease transmitted primarily by sexual activity.

syndrome: A group of symptoms that together are indicative of a specific disease.

vaccine: A preparation that is normally injected or taken orally to stimulate the immune system to be capable of fighting off an infection by a specific pathogen at a later time, thereby conferring immunity against that pathogen.

viral load: The number of viral particles that are present in a person's body.

virus: The smallest known infectious organism, causing the STDs genital herpes, AIDS, genital warts, and hepatitis B.

Organizations to Contact

Planned Parenthood Federation of America
810 Seventh Ave.
New York, NY 10019
(212) 541-7800
fax: (212) 245-1845
www.plannedparenthood.org
communications@ppfa.org
This organizaton is involved in all aspects of improving human sexual health from education and research to providing health care services for all Americans.

CDC National AIDS/HIV Hotline
P.O. Box 13827
Research Triangle Park, NC 27709
(800) 342-AIDS
www.ashastd.org
The Centers for Disease Control and Prevention can supply the most up-to-date information on HIV infection and treatments.

Sexuality Information and Education Council of the United States (SIECUS)
1706 R St. NW
Washington, DC 20009
(202) 265-2406
fax: (202) 462-2340
www.siecus.org
Promotes comprehensive education about sexuality and practices that prevent the spread of STDs.

For Further Reading

Books

Michael J. Basso, *The Underground Guide to Teenage Sexuality: An Essential Handbook for Today's Teens & Parents*. Fairview, 1997. A straightforward guide that discusses all issues of sexuality, including a chapter devoted to STDs. It includes an excellent glossary and clear illustrations.

Jean Fiedler and Hal Fiedler, *Be Smart About Sex*. Enslow, 1990. Includes a good discussion of sexuality, AIDS, and safe sex in both scientific and slang terminology.

E. James Lieberman and Karen Lieberman Troccoli, *Like It Is: A Teen Sex Guide*. McFarland, 1998. Includes a clear discussion of STDs with excellent illustrations.

Websites

American Social Health Association (www.ashastd.org). Provides good summaries on the different types of STDs and frequently asked questions.

National Center for HIV, STD, and TB Prevention, Division of Sexually Transmitted Diseases (www.cdc.gov). Informative CDC website offers a comprehensive "Sexually Transmitted Diseases Treatment Guidelines" page.

SEX, ETC. (www.sxetc.org). A teen-produced website that answers questions on topics including love, sex, abstinence, contraceptives, AIDS, STDs, drugs and drinking, violence, and health.

teenwire.com (www.teenwire.com). Planned Parenthood created this site to provide uncensored, unbiased sexuality and sexual health information to teens. It is a private, safe atmosphere where teens can have access to reliable resources. Educators and parents are welcome to register for the newsletter published by the editors of teenwire.

Works Consulted

Books

King K. Holmes et al., *Sexually Transmitted Diseases*. New York: Mc-Graw-Hill, 1990. Thorough text that includes historical details on STDs.

Stephen A. Morse, Adele A. Moreland, and King K. Holmes, *Atlas of Sexually Transmitted Diseases and AIDS*. London: Mosby-Wolfe, 1996. Detailed reference manual with extensive clinical perspective.

Periodicals

Centers for Disease Control and Prevention, "Morbidity and Mortality Weekly Report," no. 30, June 5, 1981.

Leslie M. Kantor and William F. Bacon, "Abstinence-Only Programs Implemented Under Welfare Reform Are Incompatible with Research on Effective Sexuality education." *JAMWA*, vol. 57, no. 1, Winter 2002.

Cynthia Dailard, "Abstinence Promotion and Teen Family Planning: The Misguided Drive for Equal Funding," *Guttmacher Report on Public Policy*, February 2002.

———, "Sex Education: Politicians, Parents, Teachers and Teens," *Guttmacher Report on Public Policy*, February 2001.

Michael D. Lemonick, "Little Hope, Less Help," *Time*, July 24, 2000.

Michael Specter, "The Vaccine," *New Yorker*, February 3, 2003.

Internet Sources

Mikey Aiken, "I'm Waiting," Sex, Etc., December 16, 2001. www.sx etc.com.

Alan Guttmacher Institute, "Trend Toward Abstinence-Only Sex Ed Means Many U.S. Teenagers Are Not Getting Vital Messages About Contraception," news release, 2000. www.agi-use.org.

American Dietetic Association, "Nutrition Strategies for People Living with HIV/AIDS," 2002. www.eatright.org.

"A Painful Lesson: Anyone Can Get Herpes," Sex, Etc., Winter 1998. www.sxetc.com.

Beth Ashley, "Sexually Transmitted Disease Cases Increase," *USA Today,* February 2, 1999. www.usatoday.com.

AuRx, Inc., "AuRx Announces Presentation of One-Year Results on Its Therapeutic Vaccine for Genital Herpes," November 12, 2002. http://biz.yahoo.com.

Avert.Org, "AIDS Orphans in Africa," July 25, 2002. www.avert.org.

———, "HIV & AIDS Orphans in Africa," January 13, 2003. www.avert.org.

———, "Personal Stories of Living with HIV and AIDS," n.d. www.avert.org.

BBC News, "Cervical Cancer Vaccine Success," November 20, 2002. http://news.bbc.co.uk.

———, "Genital Herpes Vaccine Breakthrough," November 22, 2002. http://news.bbc.co.uk.

Beil, L., "Stamping Out Syphilis, Experts Hope to Wipe Out Scourge in United States," *Dallas Morning News,* August 14, 2000, HIV/AIDS Resource Center of JAMA Online, www.ama-assn.org.

Dennis Blakeslee, "Microbicides: An Idea Whose Time Is . . . Coming," JAMA Newsline, November 5, 1999. www.ama-assn.org.

Paul D. Blumenthal, "Immunization Against Cervical Cancer: Who? When? Where?" *Medscape Women's Health Journal,* November 11, 2002. www.medscape.com.

Darlene Bouse, "Damaged Goods," HIV—First Person, AEGIS, November 3, 2002. www.aegis.com.

Linda Carroll, "Adam: A Man's Guide to Sexual Health," MSNBC News, September 3, 2000. www.msnbc.com.

Jonathan Cedeno, "Feel Like You're the Last American Virgin? (You're Not)," Sex, Etc., December 17, 2001. www.sxetc.com.

Centers for Disease Control and Prevention, "CDC Issues New Report on STD Epidemics," press release, December 5, 2000. www.cdc.gov.

Claudine Chamberlain, "Herpes on the Rise," ABC News, November 26, 1997. http://more.abcnews.go.com.

Chris, "To Work or Not to Work," HIV/AIDS Positive Stories, November 3, 2002. www.hivaids.webcentral.com.au.

Jeffrey P. Cohn, "The Beginnings: Laboratory and Animal Studies." *FDA Consumer Special Report,* January 1995. www.fda.gov.

Family Health International, "Opinion: Policymaking and ARVs: A Framework for Rational Decision Making," *Impact on HIV,* volume 1, no. 1, October 1998. www.fhi.org.

Gloria Feldt, "Abstinence-Only Education Is Irresponsible (and Dangerous)," speech at Yale Political Union, April 8, 2002. www.planned parenthood.org.

John Henkel, "Attacking AIDS with a 'Cocktail' Therapy," *FDA Consumer Magazine,* July–August 1999. www.fda.gov.

International AIDS Vaccine Initiative, "HIV Immunity and 'Resistant' Sex Workers: An Interview with Sarah Rowland-Jones," January–March 2000. www.iavi.org.

Kaiser Family Foundation, "National Study on Sex Education Reveals Gaps Between What Parents Want and Schools Think," news release, September 26, 2000. www.kff.org.

Kaiser Family Foundation, MTV, and *Teen People,* "What Teens Know and Don't (but Should) About Sexually Transmitted Disease: A National Survey of 15- to 17-year-olds," March 8, 1999. www.kff.org.

Annabel Kanabus, "Types, Groups and Subtypes. AIDS Vaccines," Avert. Org., August 10, 2001. www.avert.org.

Marilynn Larkin, "New STD Treatment Strategies," JAMA Women's Health STD Information Center briefing, August 3, 1998. www.ama-assn.org.

Claudio Lavanga, "Therapeutic DNA Vaccine to Be Tested in Patients with Chronic HIV Infection," *Reuters Health Information,* AIDS Meds.Com, July 10, 2002. www.aidsmeds.com.

Sharon Lerner, "An Orgy of Abstinence," *Village Voice,* August 1–7, 2001. www.villagevoice.com.

Joan Levinstein, "AIDS in Africa: Resource Center Statistics," *Time.com,* 2001. www.time.com.

Medscape, "Sexual HIV Transmission and Its Prevention; Biological HIV Prevention Strategies: Reducing Infectiousness, Susceptibility, and the Efficiency of Transmission," CME Clinical Update, June 27, 2001. www.medscape.com.

Medscape, "Sexual HIV Transmission and Its Prevention; Intervention Strategies," CME Clinical Update, June 27, 2001. www.medscape.com.

Anupama Mehta, "Messing with Myths About Genital Warts," Sex, Etc., November 22, 1998. www.sxetc.com.

David Menadue, "Is Your Future in the Stars?" *Positive Living,* August 2002, HIV/AIDS Positive Stories, November 2002. www.hiv aids.webcentral.com.au.

Milwaukee Journal Sentinel, "Many Teens Underestimate STDs," ABC News, March 8, 1999. http://more.abcnews.go.com.

Mike Mitka, "US Effort to Eliminate Syphilis Moving Forward." *JAMA,* March 22–29, 2000. http://jama.ama-assn.org.

Anne A. Oplinger, "Major Herpes Vaccine Trial Launched in Women," NIAID, news release, November 21, 2002. www.niaid.nih.gov.

Thom Pasculli, "To Be or Not to Be a Virgin? Sex is . . . Sacred," Sex, Etc., December 17, 2001. www.sxetc.com.

Sam Perdue, "NIAID Releases *The Jordan Report: Accelerated Development of Vaccines,*" NIAID, news release, August 31, 2001. www.niaid. nih.gov.

Andrea Petersen, "Overshadowed by AIDS, Herpes Spreads Alarmingly," *Wall Street Journal,* AEGIS, December 10, 1997. www.aegis.com.

David Satcher, *The Surgeon General's Call to Action to Promote Sexual Health and Responsible Sexual Behavior,* Office of the Surgeon General, June 28, 2001. www.surgeongeneral.gov.

Sonja, "Disclosure: When and How," Positive Women Victoria, HIV/AIDS Positive Stories, November 3, 2002. www.hivaids. webcentral.com.au.

Paula Span, "Living with AIDS," *Washington Post Magazine,* May 27, 2001. www.washingtonpost.com.

Joan Stephenson, "A Farewell to Harms: Experts Debate Global Disease Eradication Efforts," *JAMA,* March 25, 1998. http://jama.ama-assn.org.

———, "New Therapy Promising for Genital Herpes," *JAMA,* May 2, 2001. http://jama.ama-assn.org.

Kehinde Togun, "Living with HIV/AIDS: A Lesson in Protection," Sex Etc., August 1, 2001. www.sxetc.com.

University of Texas Medical Branch, "New Drug Reduces Frequency of Genital Herpes Flare-Ups," July 2001. www.utmb.edu.

Rebecca Vesely, "Some States Rejecting Abstinence-Only Sex Ed," Women's e NEWS, March 11, 2002. www.womensenews.org.

Village Voice, "Part 1: The Virus Creates a Generation of Orphans," November 3–9, 1999. www.villagevoice.com.

Ed Vulliamy, "Bush Promotes Virgin Values to Curb Teen Sex," *Observer,* April 28, 2002. www.observer.co.uk.

Cheryl Wetzstein, "Certain STDs Reach Highs," *Insight on the News,* November 16, 1998. www.findarticles.com.

———, "Groups Seek Abstinence-Only Curbs," *Washington Times,* September 2, 2002. www.washtimes.com.

World Health Organization, "Global Prevalence and Incidence of Selected Curable Sexually Transmitted Infections: Overview and Estimates," 2001. www.who.int.

David Wroe, "Cervical Cancer Blocked by Vaccine," *Sydney Morning Herald,* November 22, 2002. www.smh.com.au.

June Wyman, "Syphilis Genome Sequence Offers Clues to Better Diagnosis, Prevention and Treatment," NIH, news release, July 16, 1998. www.nih.gov.

Websites

Center for Disease Control's Center for HIV, STD and TB Prevention (www.cdc.gov). This site of the CDC's provides statistics, fact sheets, and prevention guidelines.

Center for Disease Control's Reproductive Health Information Source (www.cdc.gov). This site provides links to fact sheets and surveillance reports.

Columbia University's Health Question and Answer Internet Service (www.goaskalice.columbia.edu). A good source of information and answers to questions regarding STDs and other health issues.

Alan Guttmacher Institute (www.agi-usa.org). The Alan Guttmacher Institute provides access to statistics on abortion, teen pregnancy, and contraception, as well as articles from *Family Planning Perspectives, International Family Planning Perspectives,* and the *Guttmacher Report on Public Policy.*

Journal of the American Medical Association (JAMA) (http://jama.ama-assn.org). The website of the official journal of the AMA covers recent breakthroughs in treatment and research.

Kaiser Family Foundation (www.kff.org). The Kaiser Family Foundation publishes the Daily Reproductive Health Report, as well as numerous studies and surveys related to sexual and reproductive health and policy.

National Institutes of Health (NIH) (www.nih.gov). Press releases and reports on the latest medically related scientific research.

National Institute of Allergies and Infectious Diseases (www.niaid.nih.gov). A good source for up-to-date information on medical research and disease statistics.

Planned Parenthood Federation of America (www.plannedparenthood.org). This site provides access to PPFA press releases, fact sheets, historical timeline, teenwire, *Educator's Update,* and more.

San Francisco AIDS Foundation (www.sfaf.org). An excellent site that explains all topics relating to HIV infection in a reader-friendly format.

Index

Picture Credits

About the Author

Tassia Kolesnikow received a bachelor of science degree from the University of California at Los Angeles. She continued her studies at UCLA in the Department of Microbiology and Molecular Genetics, where she completed a Ph.D. and met her husband, a visiting postdoctoral fellow from Australia.

Tassia moved to Sydney, Australia, in 1994 to participate in research on *Helicobacter pylori,* a bacterium that infects the human stomach and causes ulcers and cancer. She has authored numerous scientific articles and edited a book on the topic of *H. pylori.* In addition, Tassia has developed a series of highly successful workshops to introduce grade school and high school students to the wonders of molecular biology. These were featured in two episodes of the children's science show *Totally Wild,* which aired on Australian National Television.

Tassia currently lectures at the University of New South Wales in Sydney and works as a scientific consultant and writer, creating science-oriented children's books in her spare time. Tassia enjoys scuba diving and overnight bushwalks in the many wild regions of Australia with her husband and two sons.